W0081503

Official Cambridge Exam Preparation

Kid's Box

New Generation

British English

Caroline Nixon &
Michael Tomlinson

Starter

S

Class Book with Digital Pack

CAMBRIDGE

Language summary

	Key vocabulary	Key language and functions	Sounds
1 Hello! page 4	**Character names:** Marie, Maskman, Monty **Numbers:** one, two, three, four, five, six	Hello! Goodbye. What's your name? I'm (Marie). How old are you? I'm (six).	May, mouse, Matt, Monty, Maskman, Marie page 10
2 My class page 12	**Classroom objects:** bag, book, chair, eraser, pencil, table	**Classroom language:** open your books, close your books, stand up, sit down, listen, look, point What's this? It's a (pencil).	cat, black, bag page 18
page 20	**Marie's maths** **What shapes can I see?** **Shapes:** circle, triangle, square		
page 22	**Maskman's practice** units 1 and 2		
page 24	**Trevor's values** **Asking nicely**	Pass me the …, please. Here you are. Thank you.	
page 25	**Review** units 1 and 2		
3 My colours page 26	**Colours:** black, blue, brown, red, white, yellow	It's (red). It's a (red) (pencil). What's your favourite colour? It's (yellow).	brown, bear, blue, bag, black, book page 32
4 My toys page 34	**Toys:** ball, bike, car, doll, kite, robot	Where's the (car)? It's here.	cat, black, bike, cow, car, kite page 40
page 42	**Marie's art** **What is symmetry?** **Colours:** orange, green, pink **Objects:** butterfly, flower, train	Is it symmetrical? Yes, it is. No, it isn't.	
page 44	**Maskman's practice** units 3 and 4		
page 46	**Trevor's values** **Giving** Mummy, Daddy	Here's a … for you.	
page 47	**Review** units 3 and 4		

1 Hello!

1 2–3 **Listen and point. Listen and repeat.**

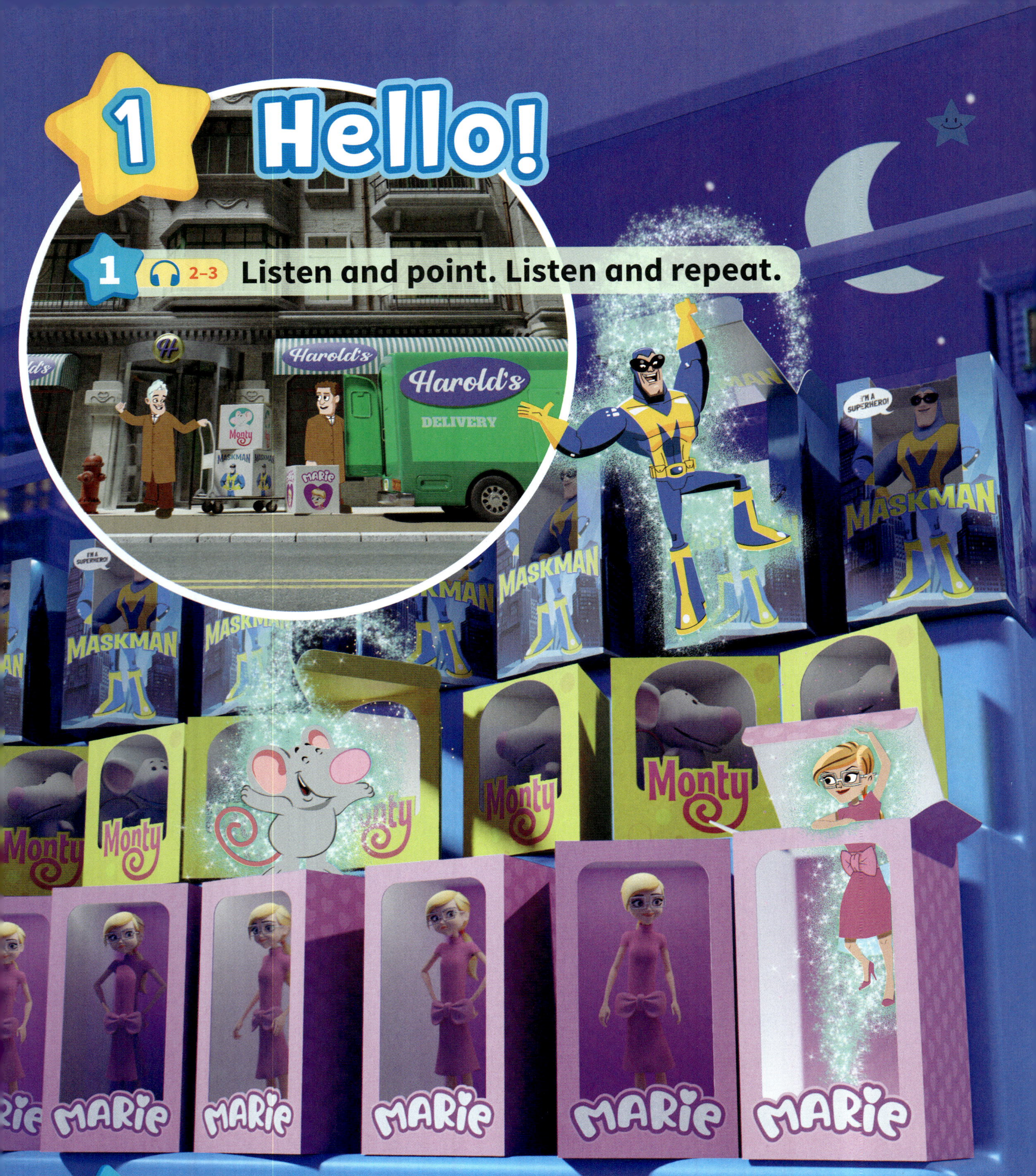

2 4 **Say the chant. Do the actions.**

Vocabulary presentation: names and numbers 1–3

1 Listen and tick (✓). 5

1

2

3

4

2 Look and draw. Say the number.

1

3	1	2
3	3	1
2	1	3

2

1	3	2
3	2	2
3	1	2

3

2	3	1
3	1	2
1	1	3

4

2	1	1
1	3	2
3	3	3

Do the online activities on Practice Extra as you complete this unit.

1 Listen and point. Sing the song. 6

2 Ask and answer.

How old are you?

I'm five.

1 Look and draw. Say the numbers.

2	6	3
5	1	4

2 8 Listen and circle.

1

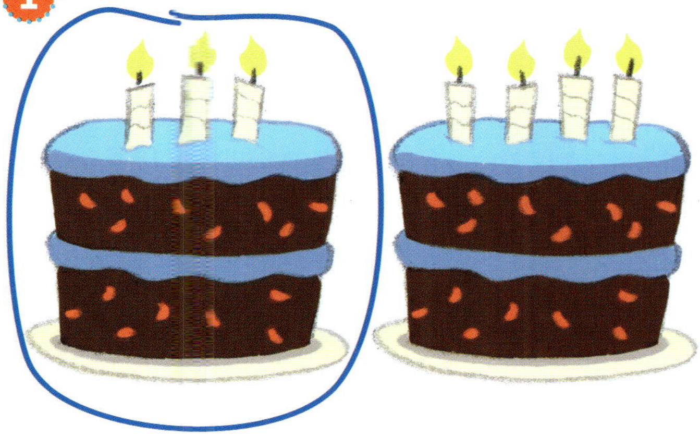

2

3

4

1 9 Watch the video. Listen and act out the story.

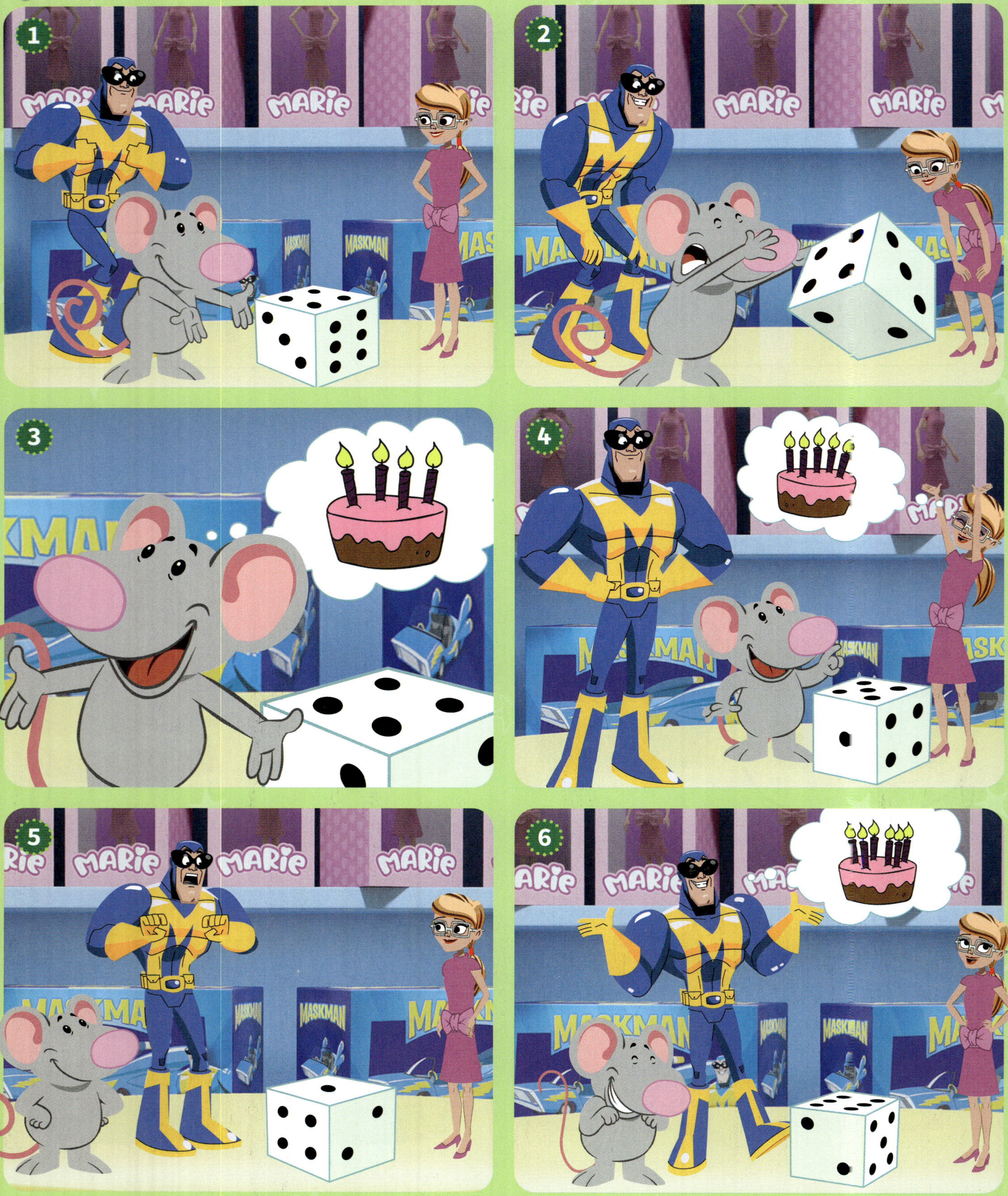

1 10 Listen and circle. Who says it?

1

2

3

4

2 Play and draw.

How old are you?

I'm four.

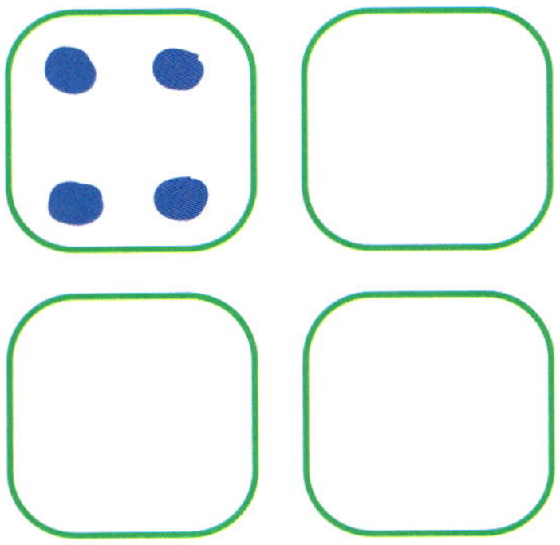

Monty's sounds

1 11 **Watch and say.**

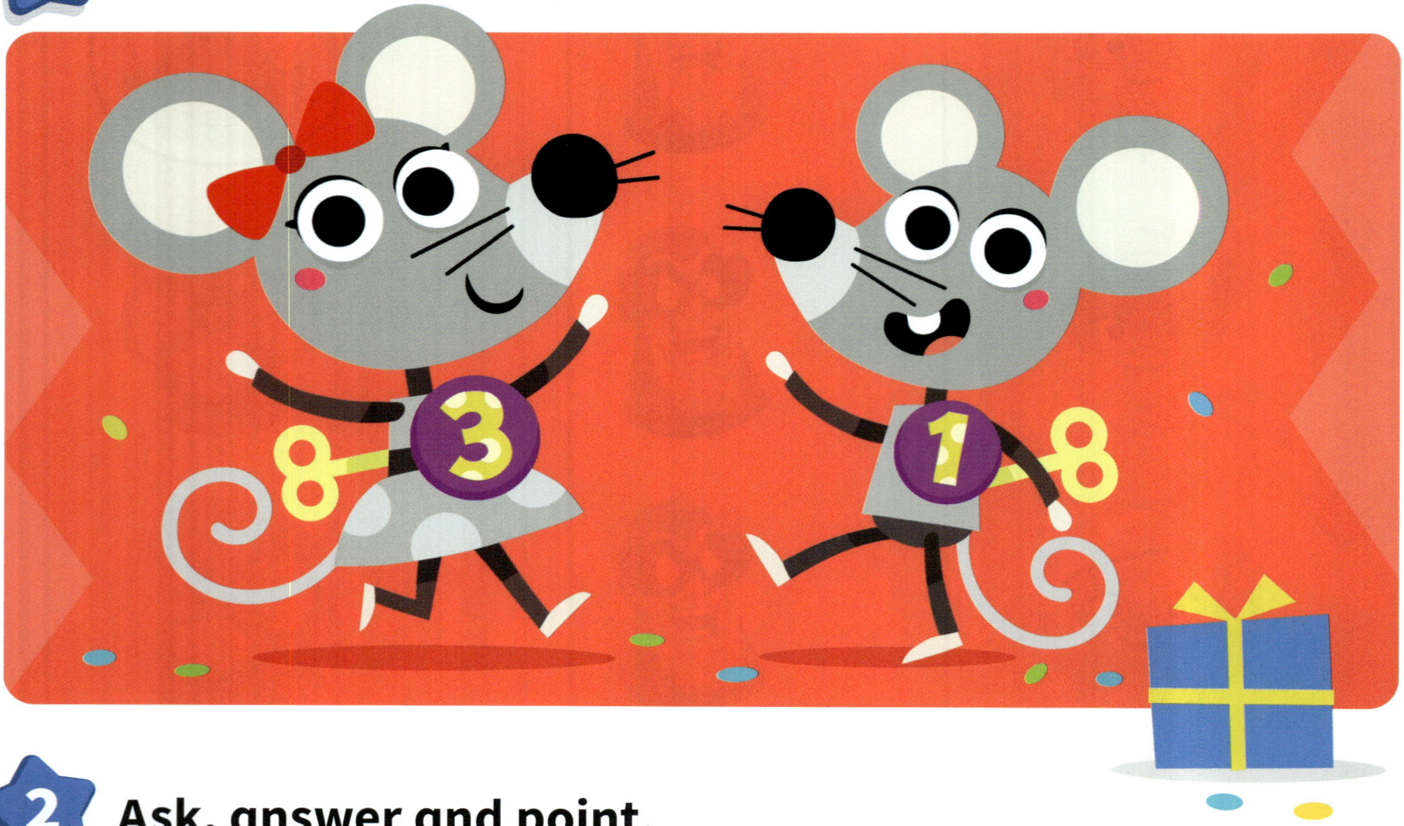

2 **Ask, answer and point.**

What's your name?

I'm Matt Mouse.

How old are you?

I'm one.

Sounds: <u>M</u>ay, <u>m</u>ouse, <u>M</u>att, <u>M</u>onty, <u>M</u>askman, <u>M</u>arie

1 12 Listen and stick.

2 13 Talk to Maskman.

2 My class

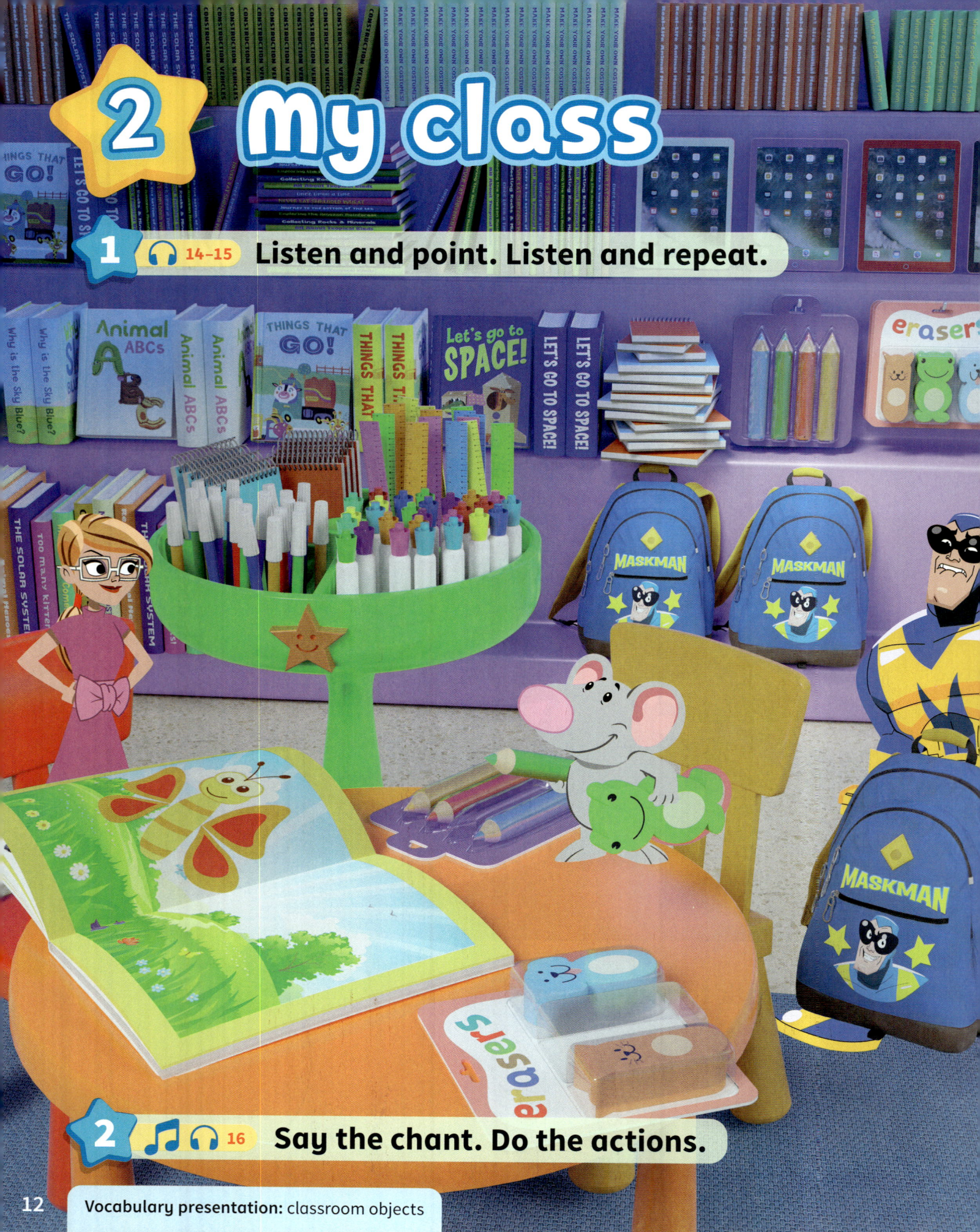

1 14–15 **Listen and point. Listen and repeat.**

2 16 **Say the chant. Do the actions.**

1 17 Listen and circle the number.

1

4 5

2

2 3

3
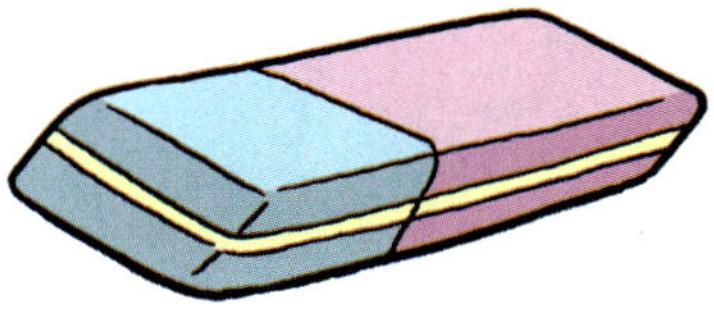
3 4

4

2 3

5

5 6

6

1 2

2 Look and complete.

1

?

2

?

3

?

1 18 Listen and point. Sing the song.

2 Say and do.

1 2C Listen and tick (✓).

1

2

3

4

2 Draw your classroom. Say.

Me!

1 21 **Watch the video. Listen and act out the story.**

1 Listen and write the number.

22

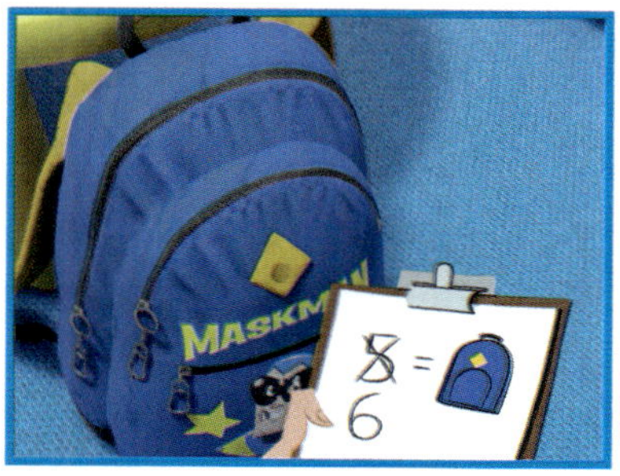

1

2 Circle. Say and circle.

Three tables.

Yes, three tables.

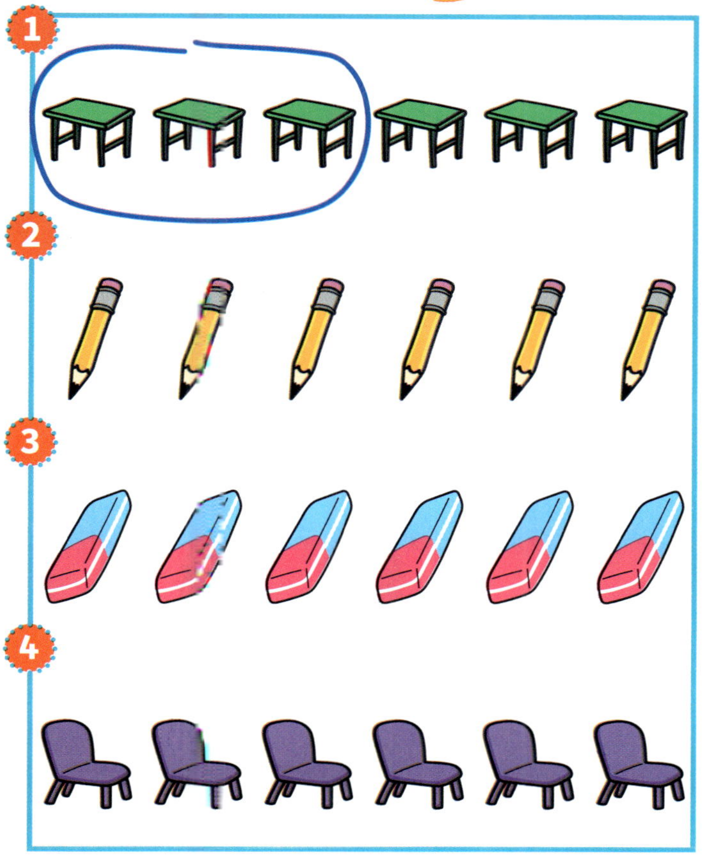

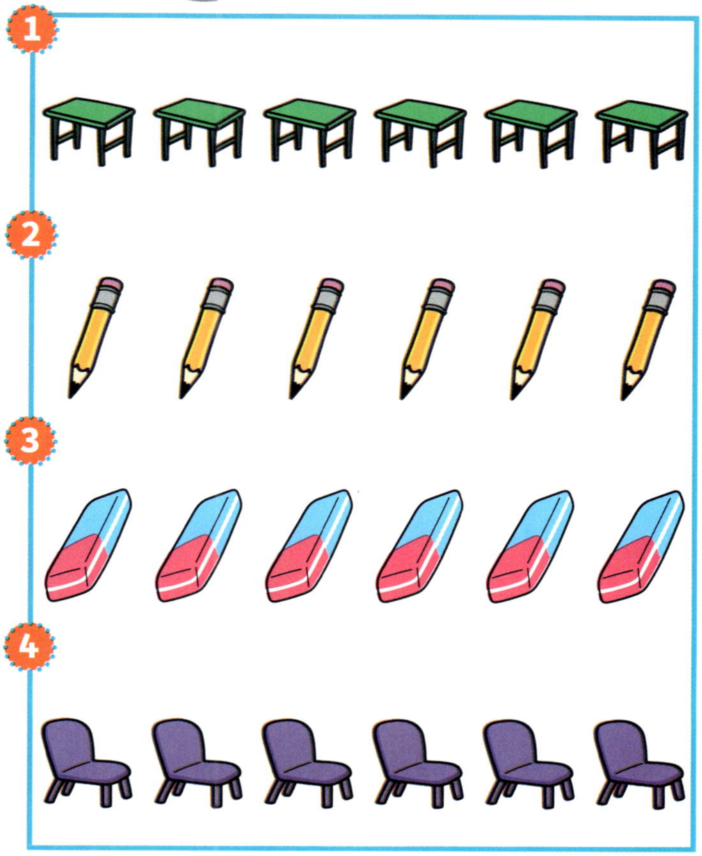

Monty's sounds

1 23 Watch and say.

2 Ask and answer.

What's your name?

I'm Alice Cat.

Sounds: *cat*, *black*, *bag*

1 24 Listen and stick.

2 25 Talk to Maskman.

Marie's maths

What shapes can I see?

1 Watch the video. Answer.

2 26 Listen and point. Say the shapes.

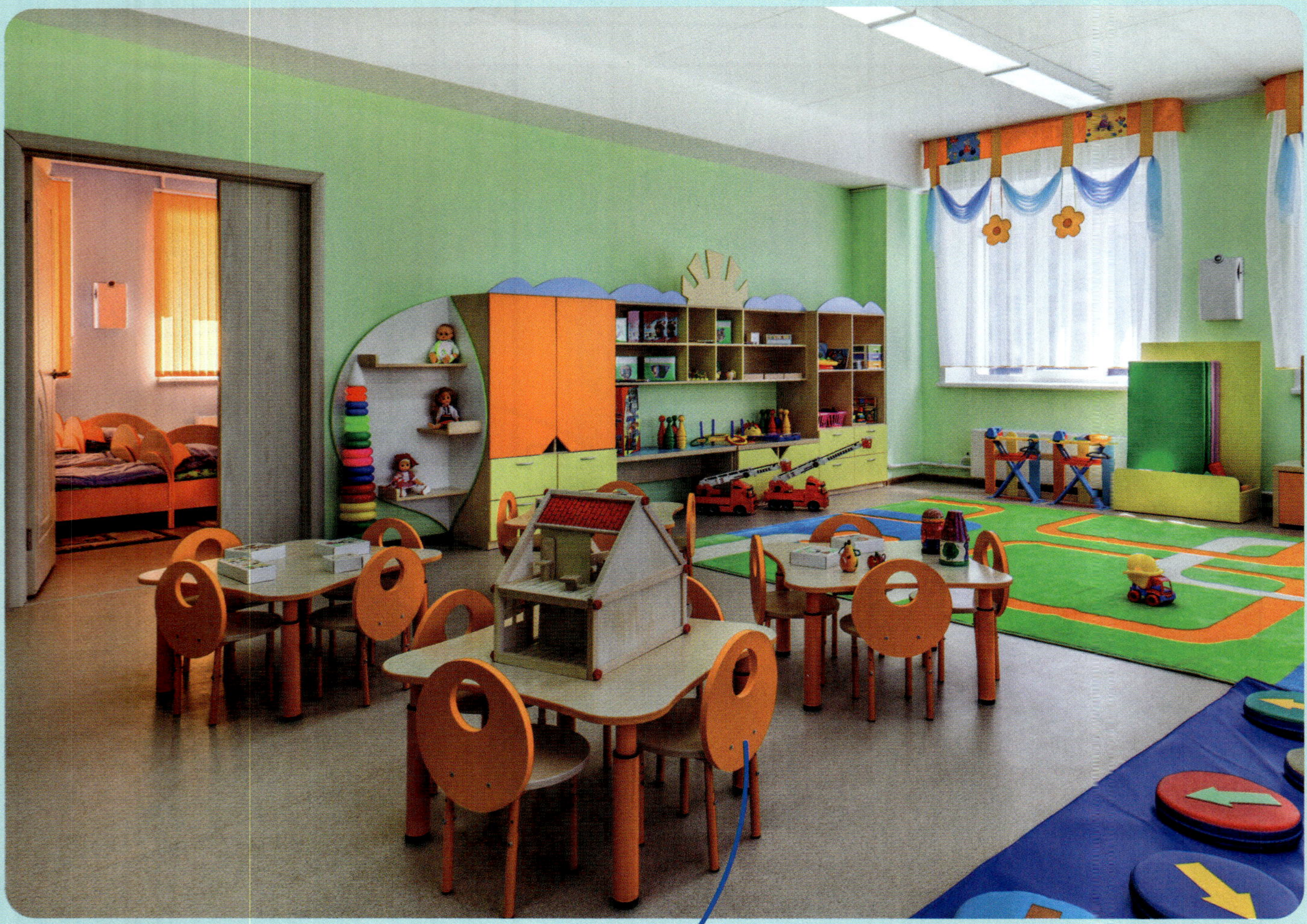

3 Look and draw lines.

4 2 Listen and look. Count and write.

1

3

2

3

5 Look and draw. Colour.

1
2
3
4

Project

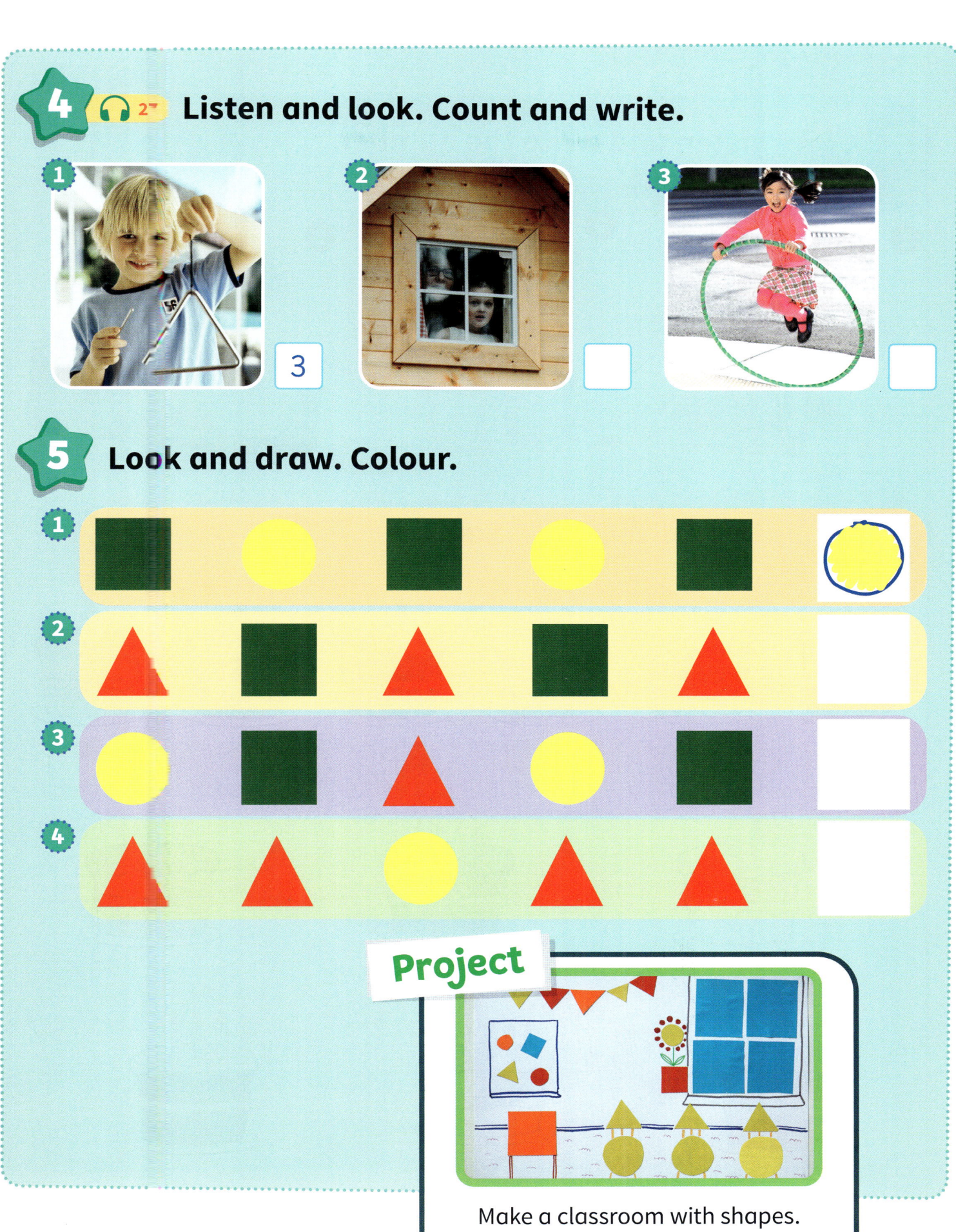

Make a classroom with shapes.

Maskman's practice

1 28 **Listen and write the number. Act it out.**

2 **Count and draw lines. Say.**

3 29 Look and count. Listen and circle.

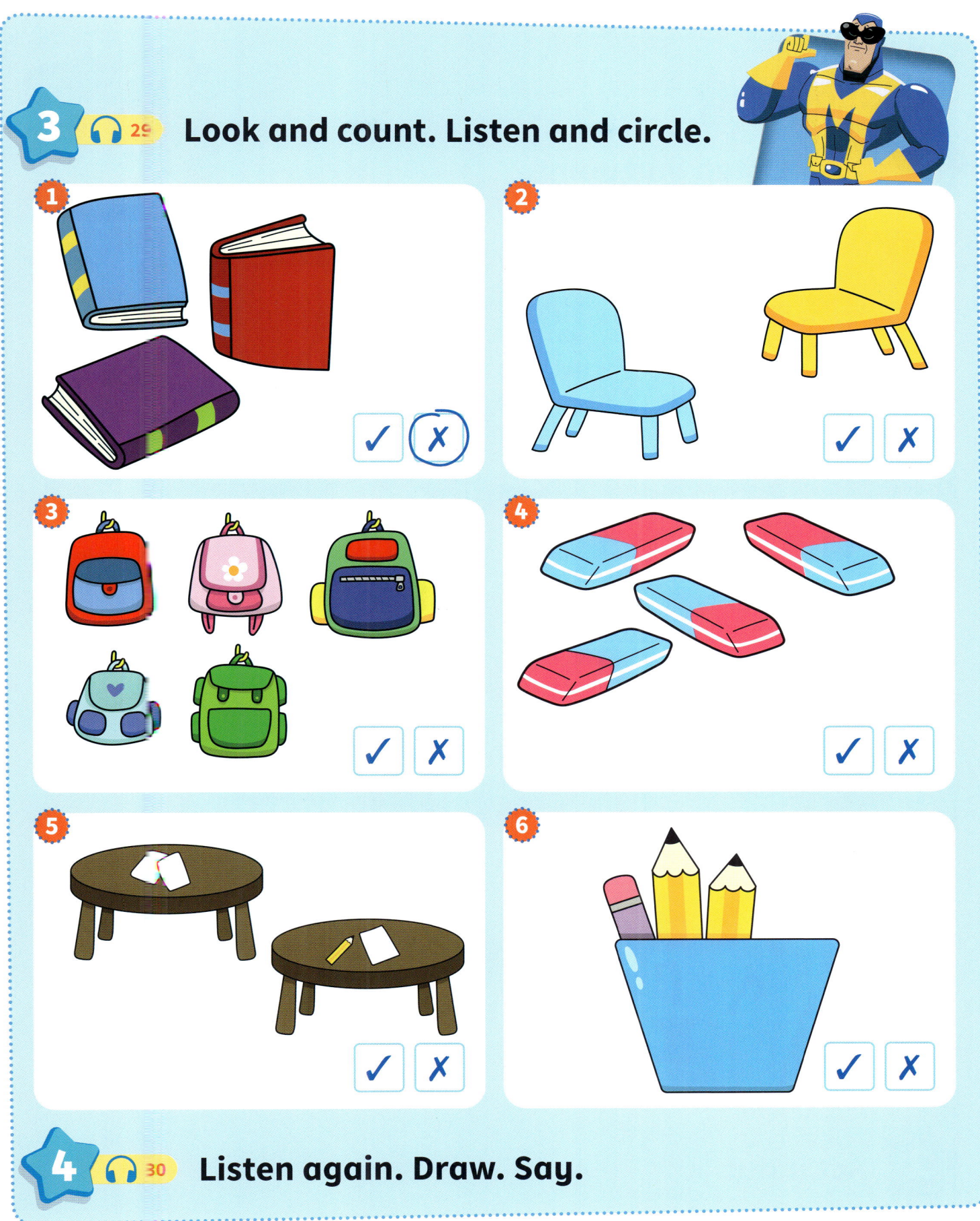

1

✓ ✗

2

✓ ✗

3

✓ ✗

4

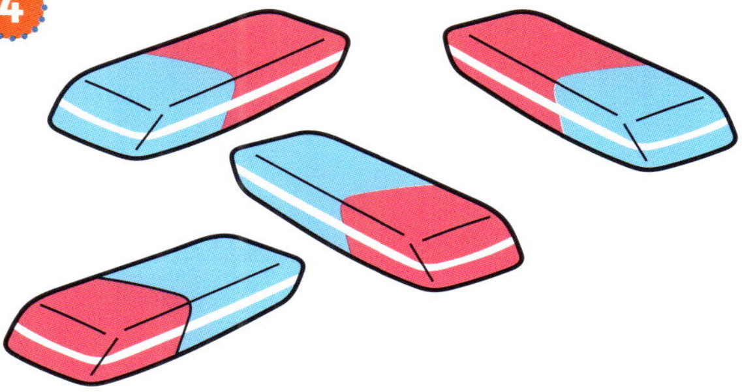

✓ ✗

5

✓ ✗

6

✓ ✗

4 30 Listen again. Draw. Say.

Trevor's values

Asking nicely

1 31 **Listen and point.**

2 **Act it out.**

Asking nicely: *Pass me the pencil, please. Here you are. Thank you.* | social responsibilities

Review Units 1 and 2

1 32 Listen and circle the number.

1

5 6

2

2 3

3

3 4

4

1 2

2 33 Listen, count and colour.

1

2

3

4
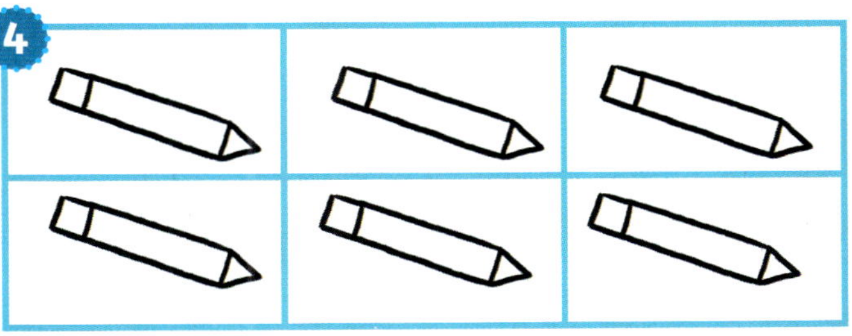

5
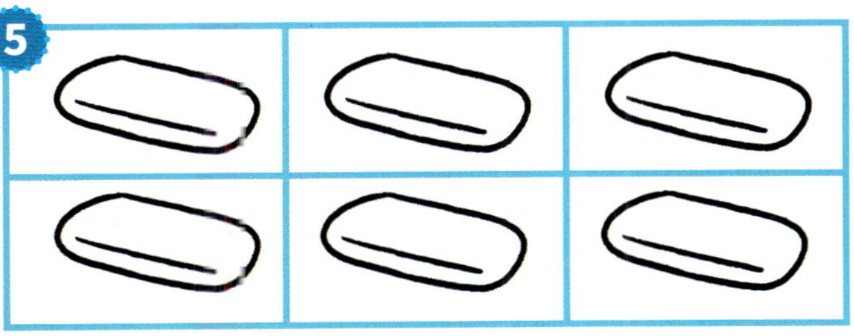

6

Remember to finish the online activities for these units on Practice Extra.

3 My colours

1 34–35 **Listen and point. Listen and repeat.**

2 36 **Say the chant. Do the actions.**

3

1 37 Listen and draw lines.

1 2 3

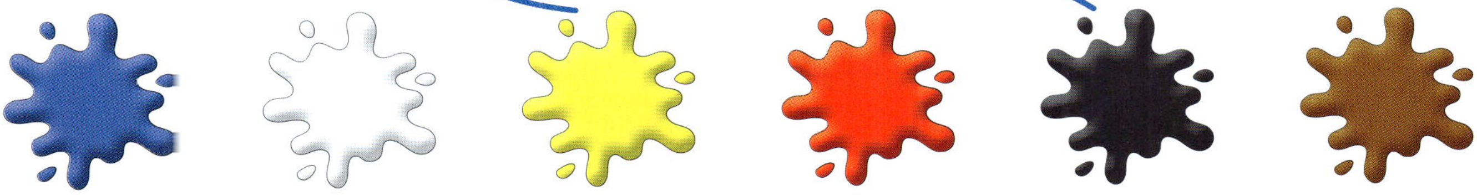

2 33 Listen and colour.

1
2
3
4
5
6

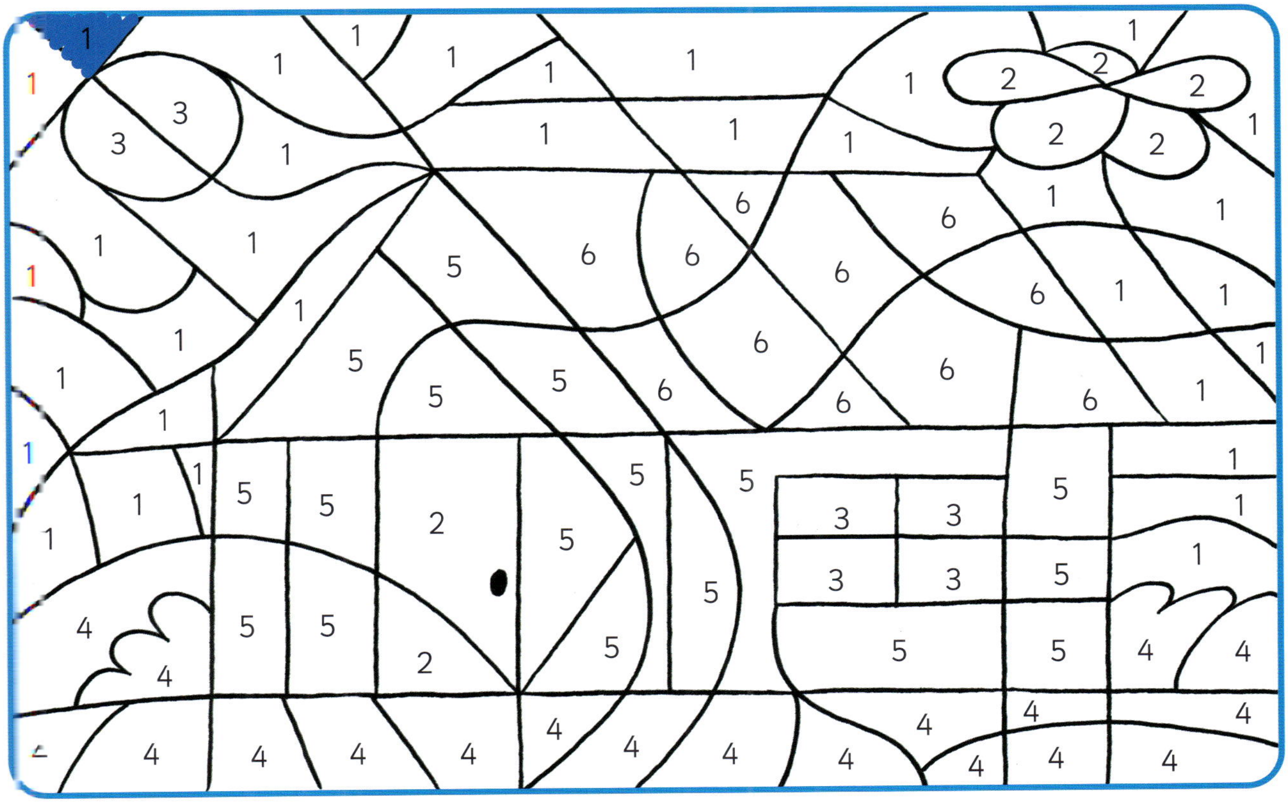

Do the online activities on Practice Extra as you complete this unit.

1 Listen and point. Sing the song.

2 Point and say.

It's a red pencil.

Language presentation: *It's a red pencil.*

1 41 Listen and colour.

1

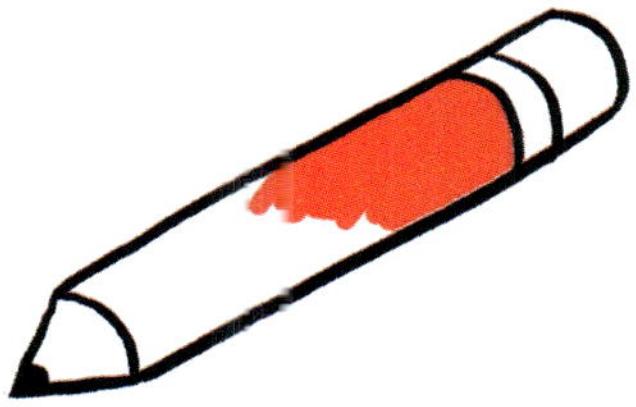

2

3

4

5

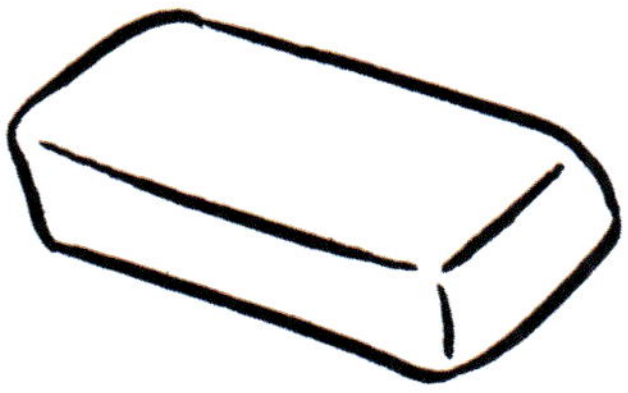

6

2 42 Listen, count and answer.

1 🎧 43 ▶ Watch the video. Listen and act out the story.

1 44 Listen and colour.

2 Colour. Say and colour.

Colour number 1 black, please.

Yes, number 1 is black.

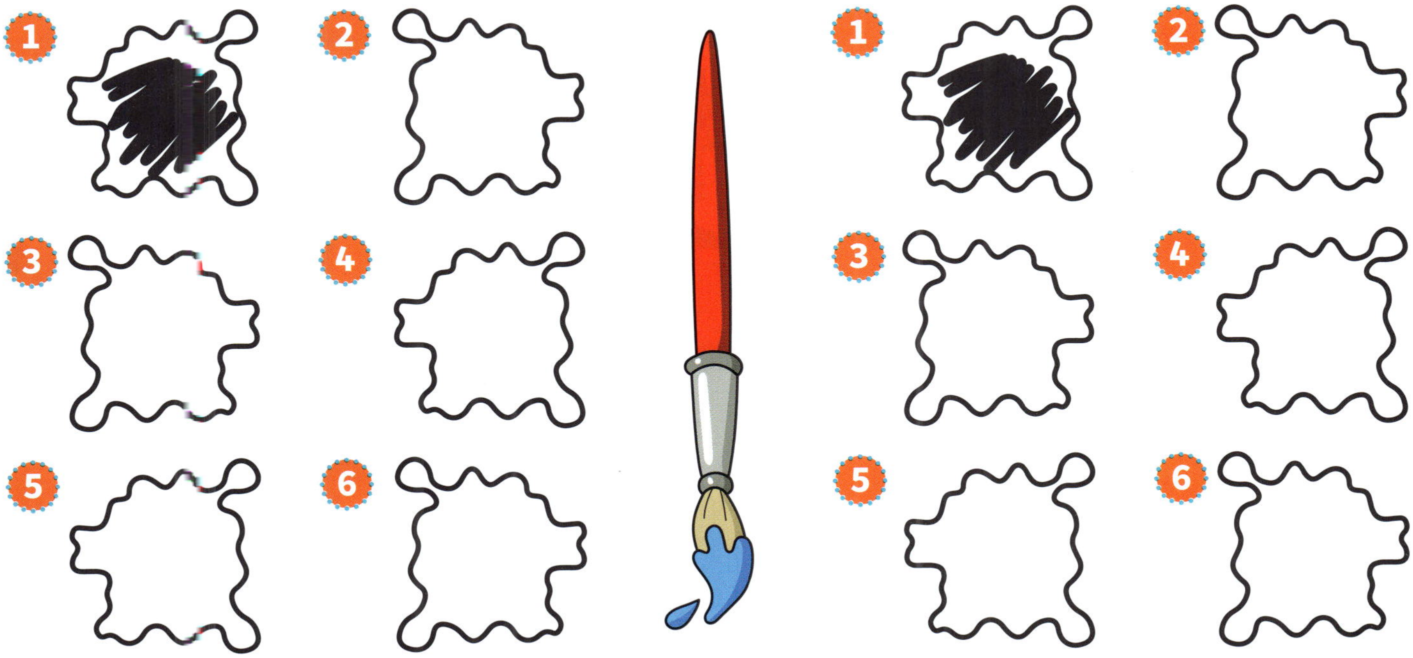

Monty's sounds

1 45 **Watch and say.**

2 **Ask and answer.**

Bears.

Six bears.

Yes!

Sounds: *<u>b</u>rown*, *<u>b</u>ear*, *<u>b</u>lue*, *<u>b</u>ag*, *<u>b</u>lack*, *<u>b</u>ook*

1 46 Listen and stick.

2 47 Talk to Maskman.

4 My toys

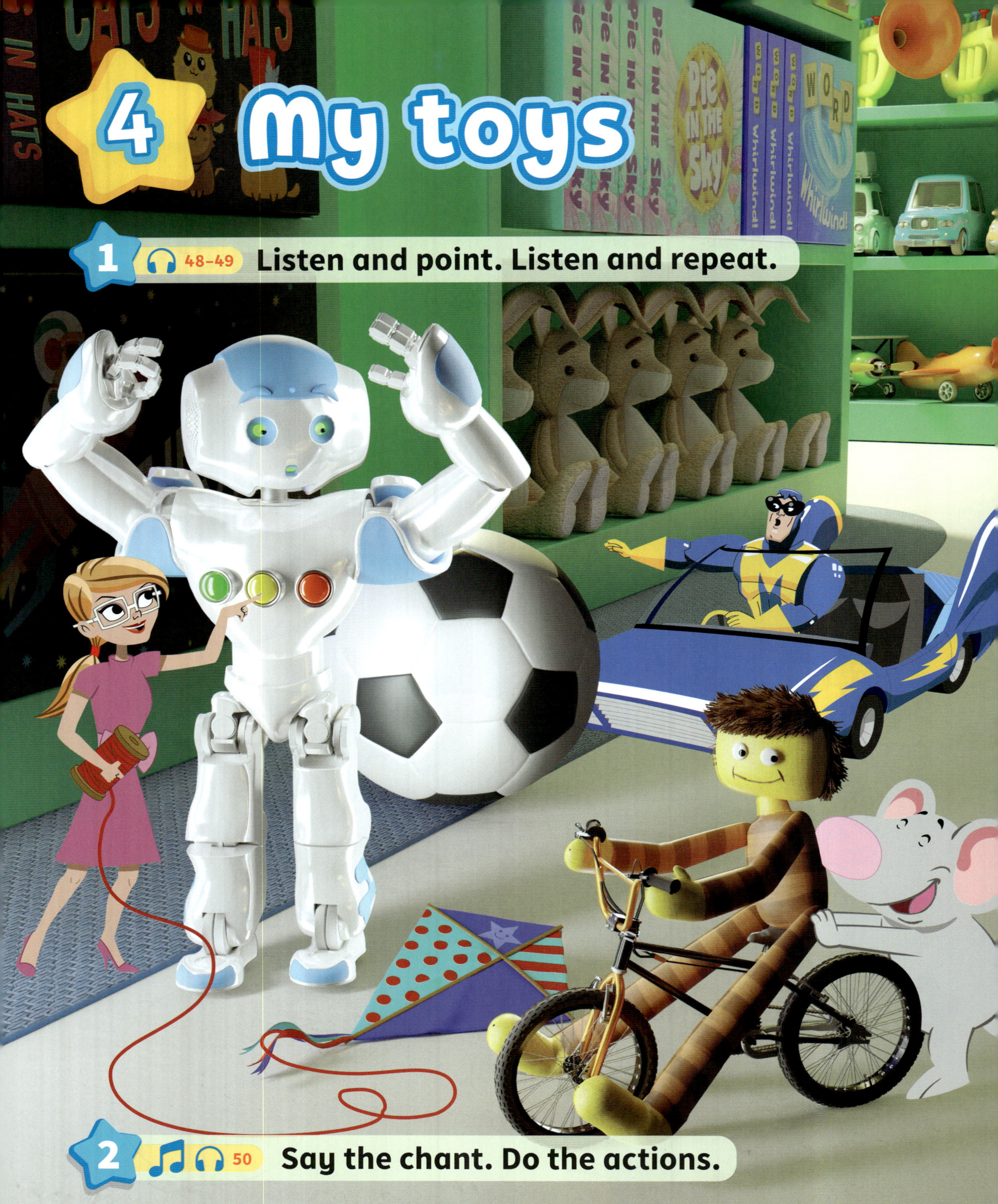

1 48–49 **Listen and point. Listen and repeat.**

2 50 **Say the chant. Do the actions.**

1 51 Listen and colour.

1

2

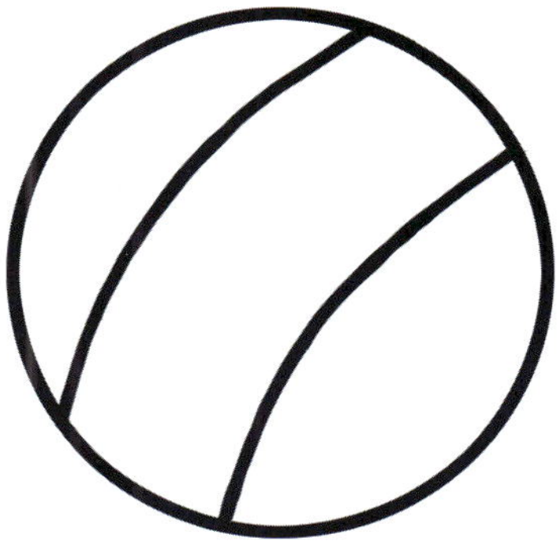

3

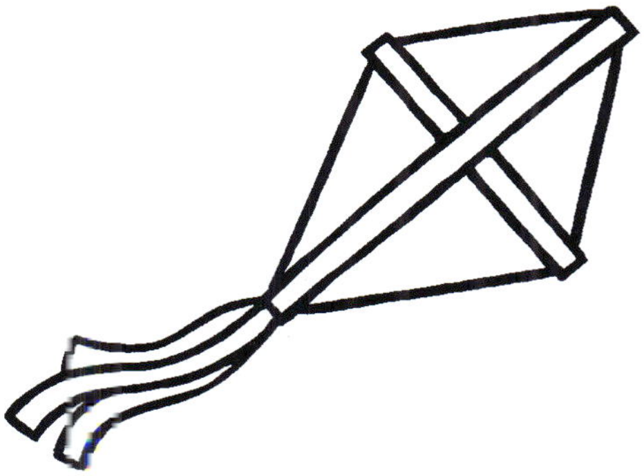

4

2 52 Listen and draw lines.

1 2 3 4

1 Listen and point. Sing the song.

2 Ask and answer.

Language presentation: *Where's the car? It's here.*

1 55 Listen and write the number.

2 Draw your favourite toy. Say.

Me!

1 56 **Watch the video. Listen and act out the story.**

Story: unit language in context

1 57 Listen and circle. Say.

1

✓ ✗

2

✓ ✗

3

✓ ✗

4

✓ ✗

5

✓ ✗

6

✓ ✗

2 Draw and colour. Ask and answer.

What's your toy?

It's a brown doll.

Monty's sounds

1 Watch and say.

58

2 Ask and answer.

Cars. Two cars. Yes!

Sounds: *cat*, *black*, *bike*, *cow*, *car*, *kite*

1 59 Listen and stick.

2 60 Talk to Maskman.

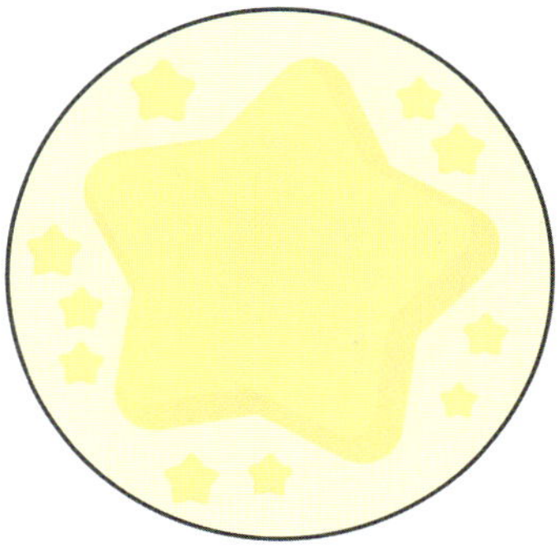

Marie's art

What is symmetry?

1 Watch the video. Answer.

2 61 Listen, point and say. Listen and colour.

1

2

3
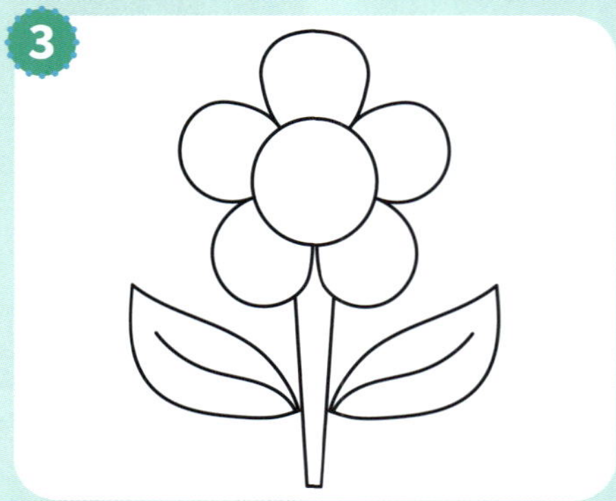

3 Look and tick (✓) or cross (✗).

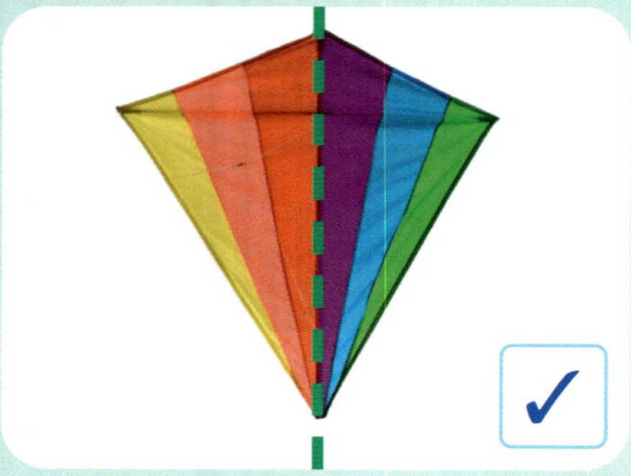

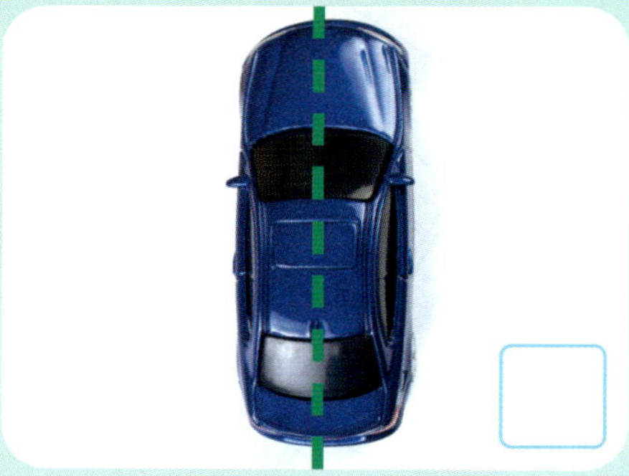

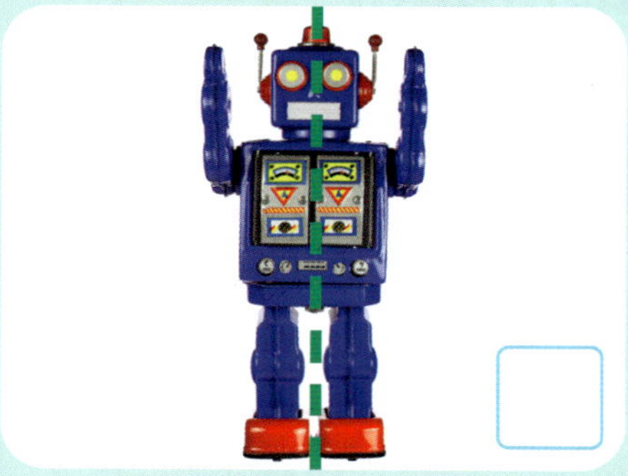

4 Look and trace. Colour and say.

1

2

5 Look and draw. Draw for your friend.

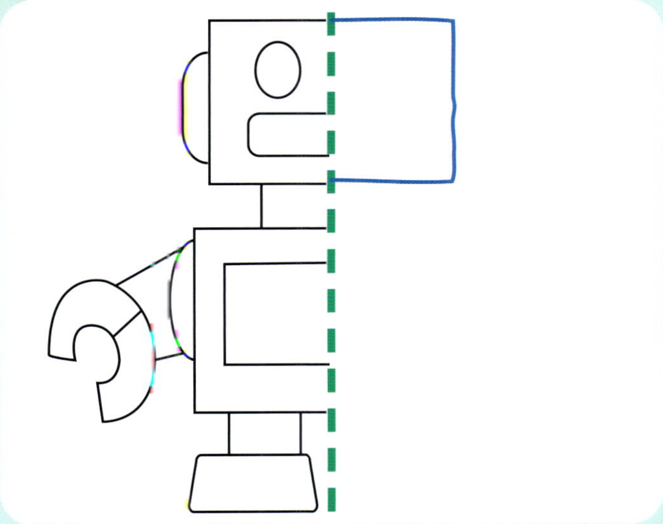

Project

Paint a symmetrical picture.

Maskman's practice

1 🎧 62 Listen and tick (✓). Act it out.

2 Count and write the number. Say.

3 63 Listen and write the number. Listen and colour.

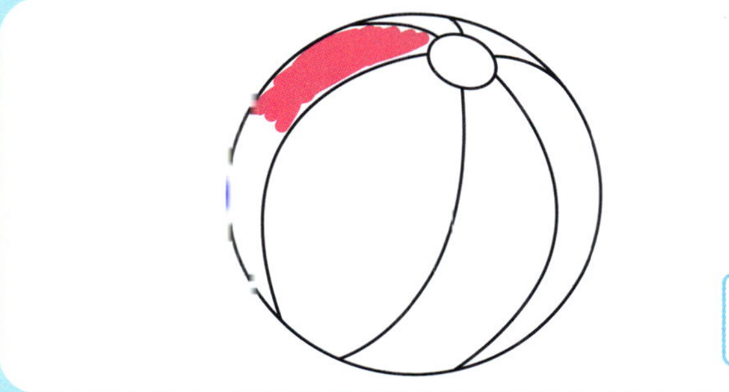

1

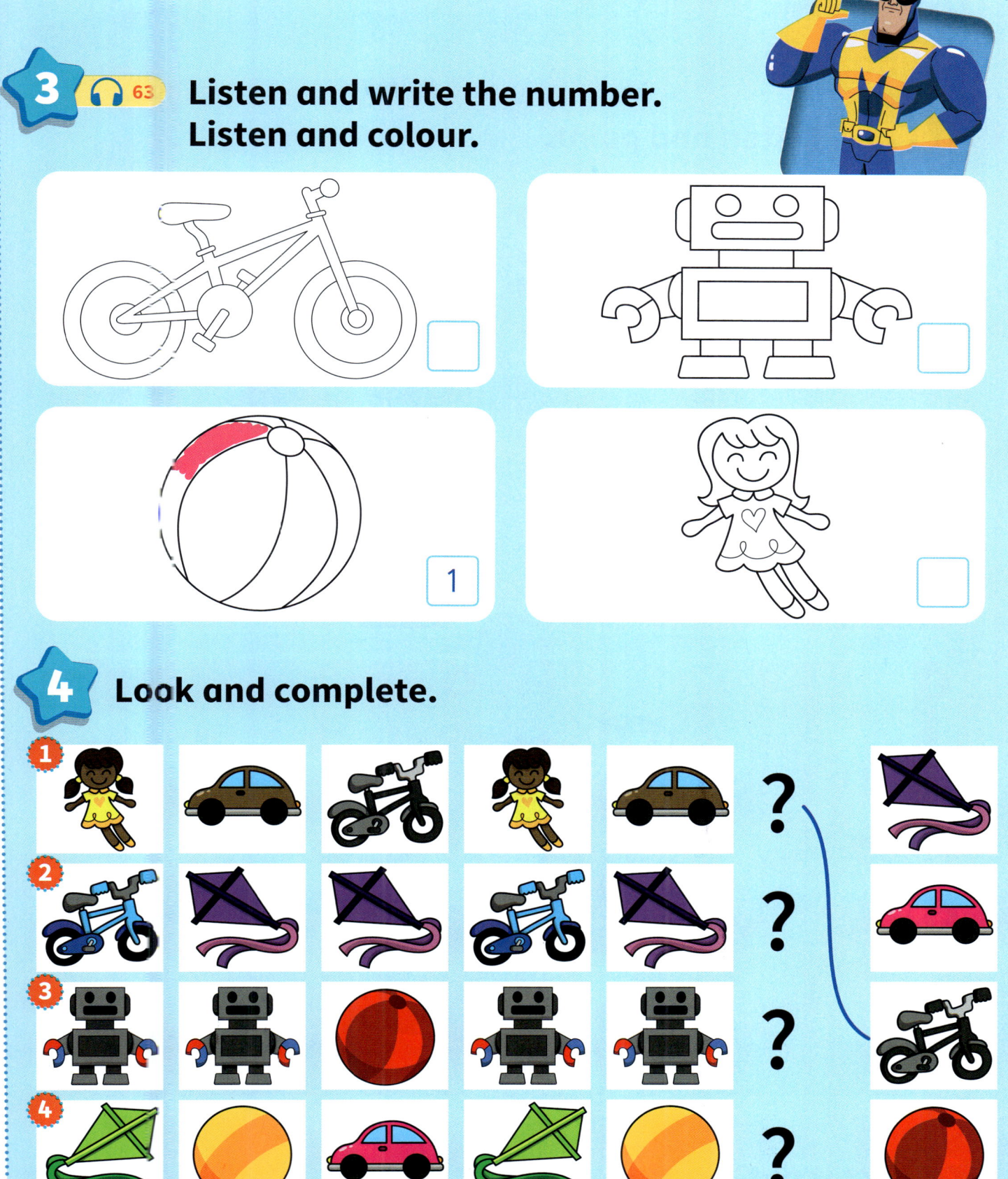

4 Look and complete.

Trevor's values

Giving

1 64 **Listen and point.**

2 **Act it out.**

Giving: *Mummy, Daddy; Here's a kite for you.* | social responsibilities

Review Units 3 and 4

1 🎧 65 Listen and colour.

1 ☐
2 ☐
3 ☐
4 ☐
5 ☐
6 ☐

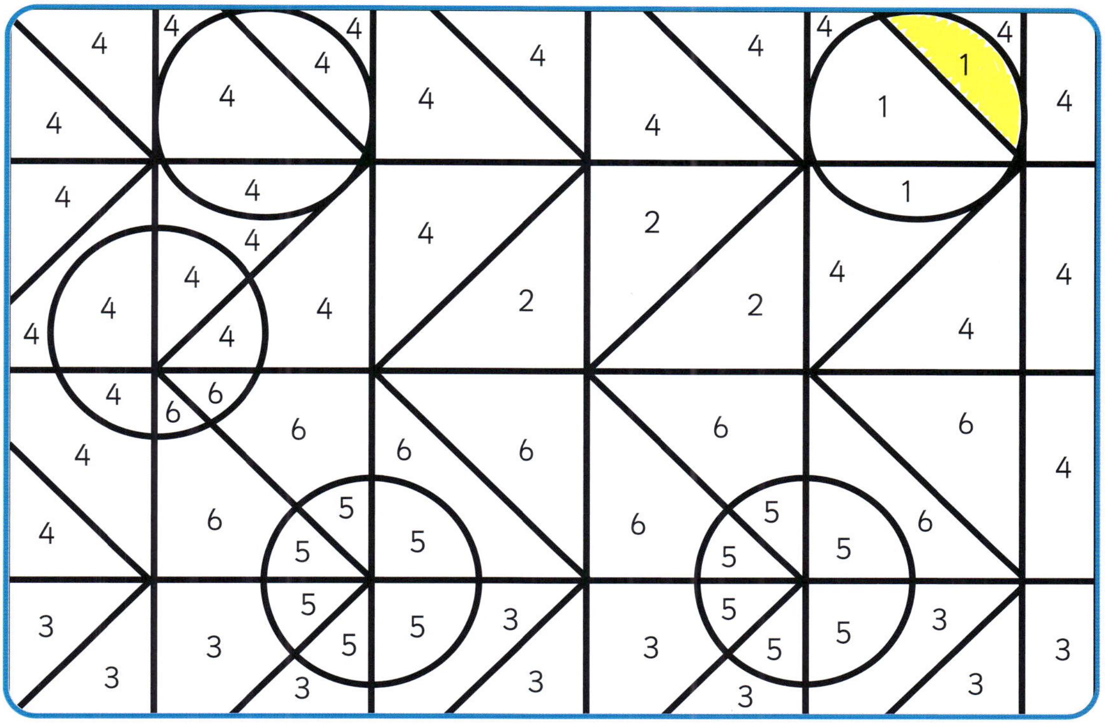

2 🎧 66 Listen and write the number.

☐

☐

☐

☐

1

☐

Remember to finish the online activities for these units on Practice Extra.

5 My house

1 67–68 **Listen and point. Listen and repeat.**

2 69 **Say the chant. Do the actions.**

1 70 Listen and circle.

1

2

3

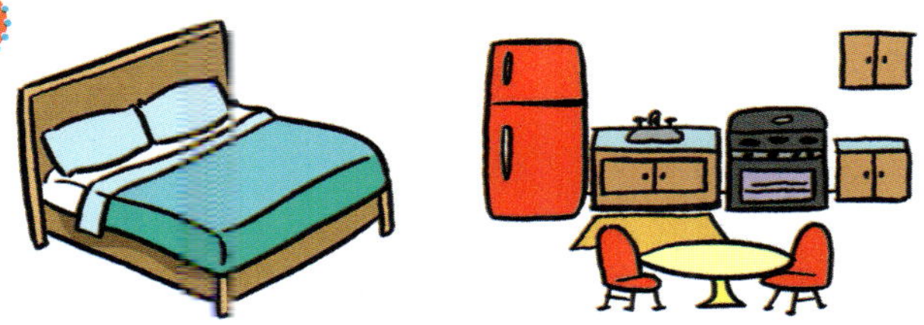

4

5

6

2 71 Listen and colour.

Do the online activities on Practice Extra as you complete this unit.

1 72 **Listen and point. Sing the song.**

2 **Say and point.**

She's in the bag.

Here!

Language presentation: *She's in the bag.*

1 74 Listen and draw lines.

2 75 Listen and follow.

1 76 Watch the video. Listen and act out the story.

1 77 Listen and draw lines.

2 Ask and answer.

Where's Maskman?

He's in the white bed.

Monty's sounds

1 78 Watch and say.

2 Ask and answer.

Where's the cat?

It's in the bedroom. It's in the bed.

Sounds: *dog*, *under*, *bed*, *duck*

1 79 Listen and stick.

2 80 Talk to Maskman.

6 My body

1 81–82 **Listen and point. Listen and repeat.**

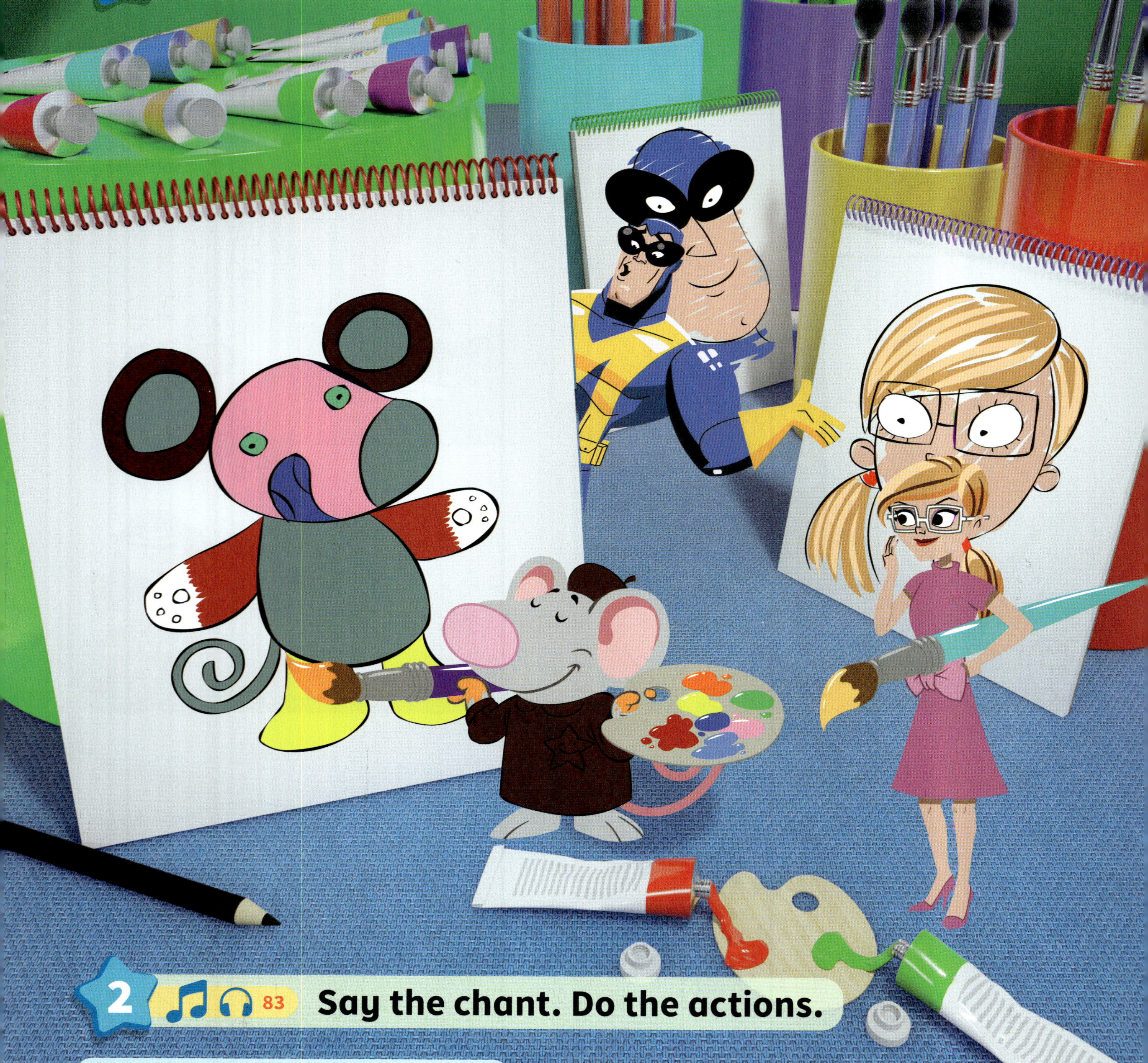

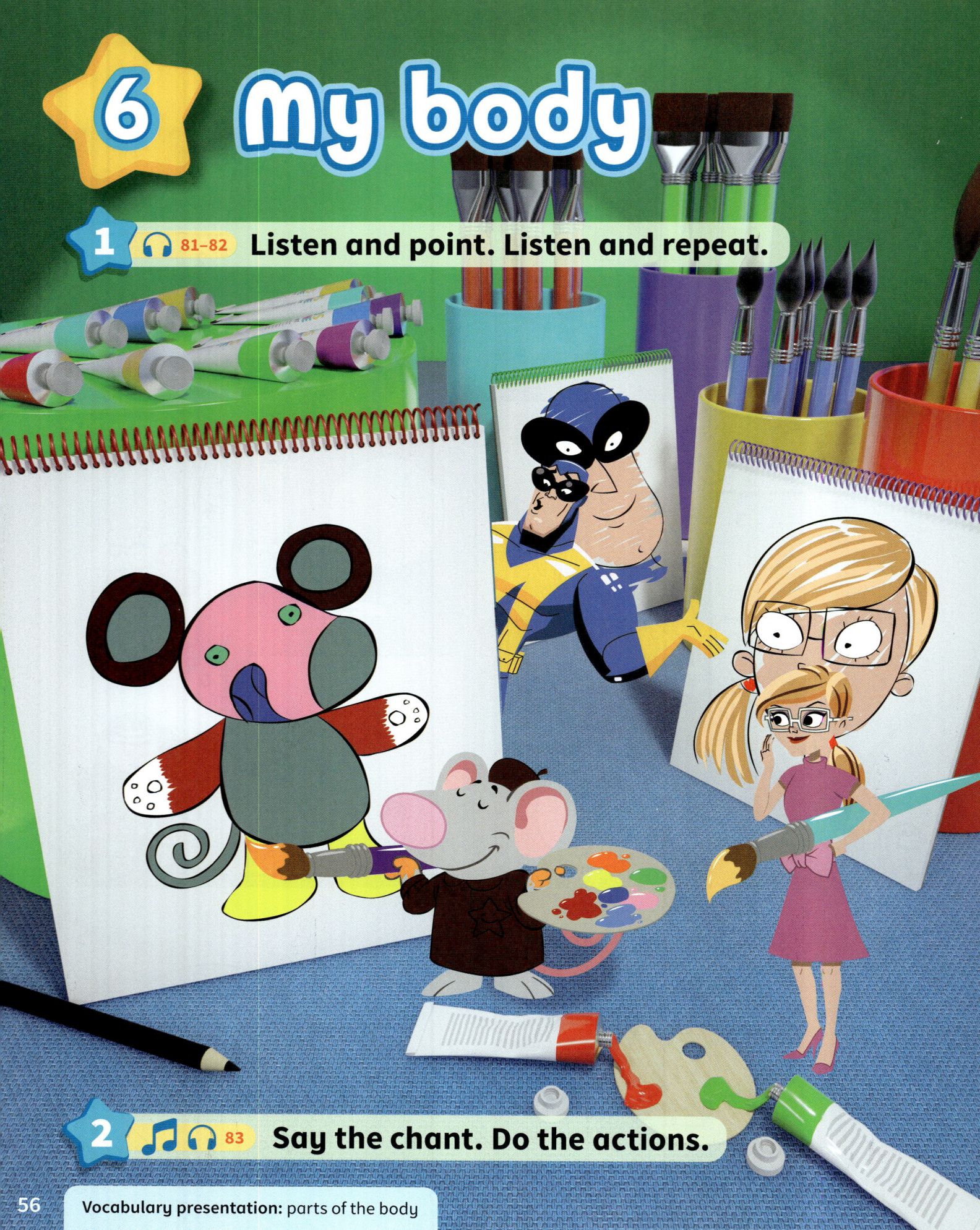

2 83 **Say the chant. Do the actions.**

1 Listen and write the number.

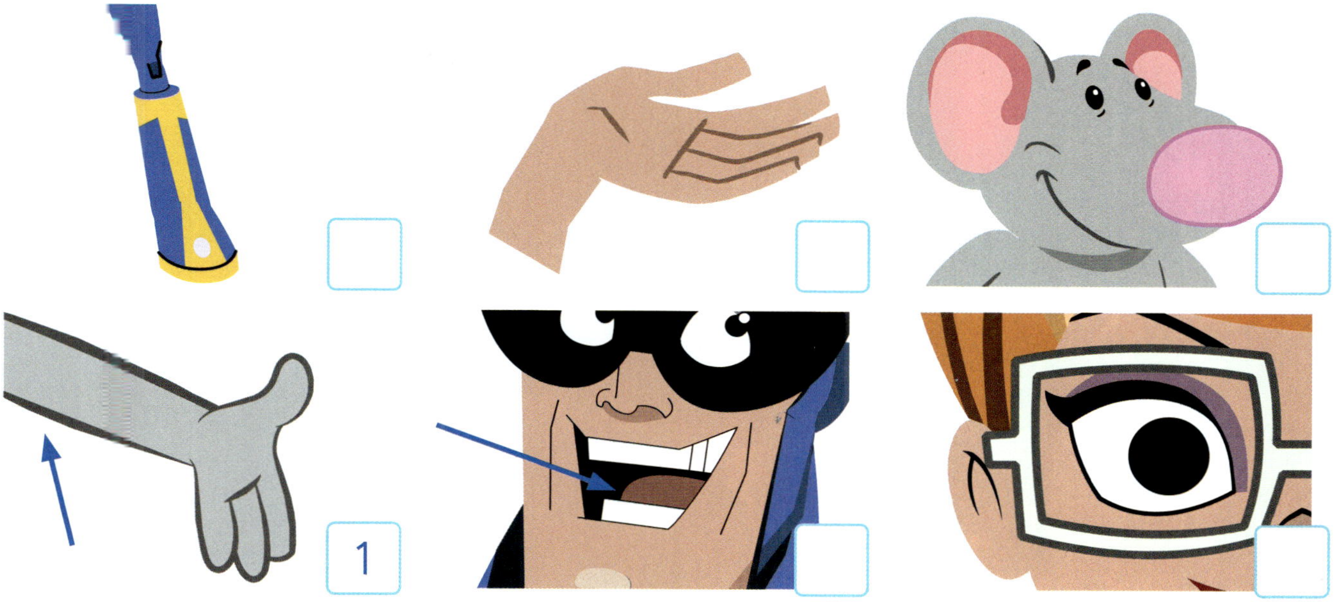

2 Look and complete.

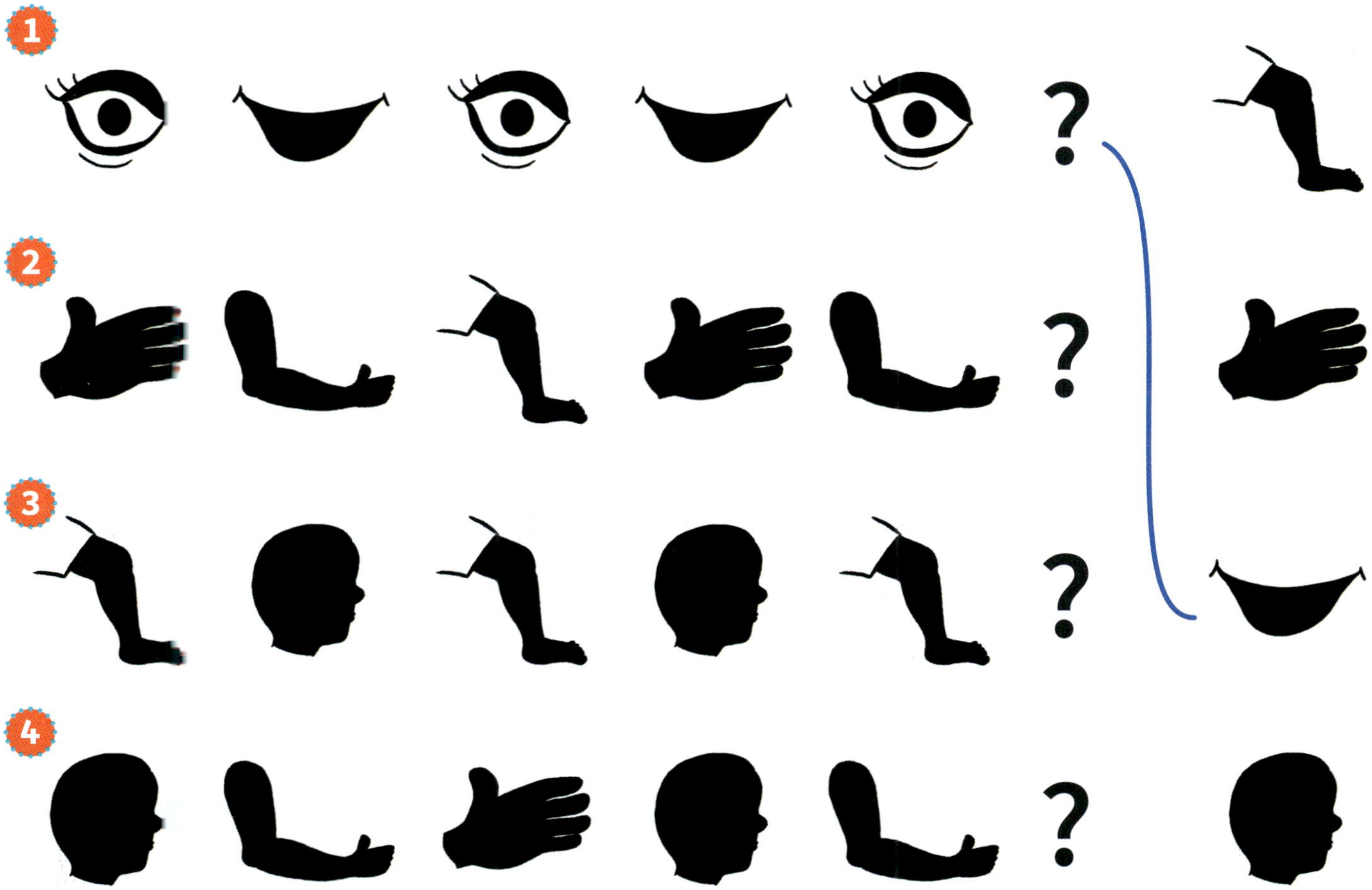

1 85 Listen and point. Sing the song.

2 Play true or false.

I've got four hands.

False!

Language presentation: *I've got four hands.*

1 87 Listen and tick (✓).

2 Draw an alien. Say.

1 🎧 88 ▶ Watch the video. Listen and act out the story.

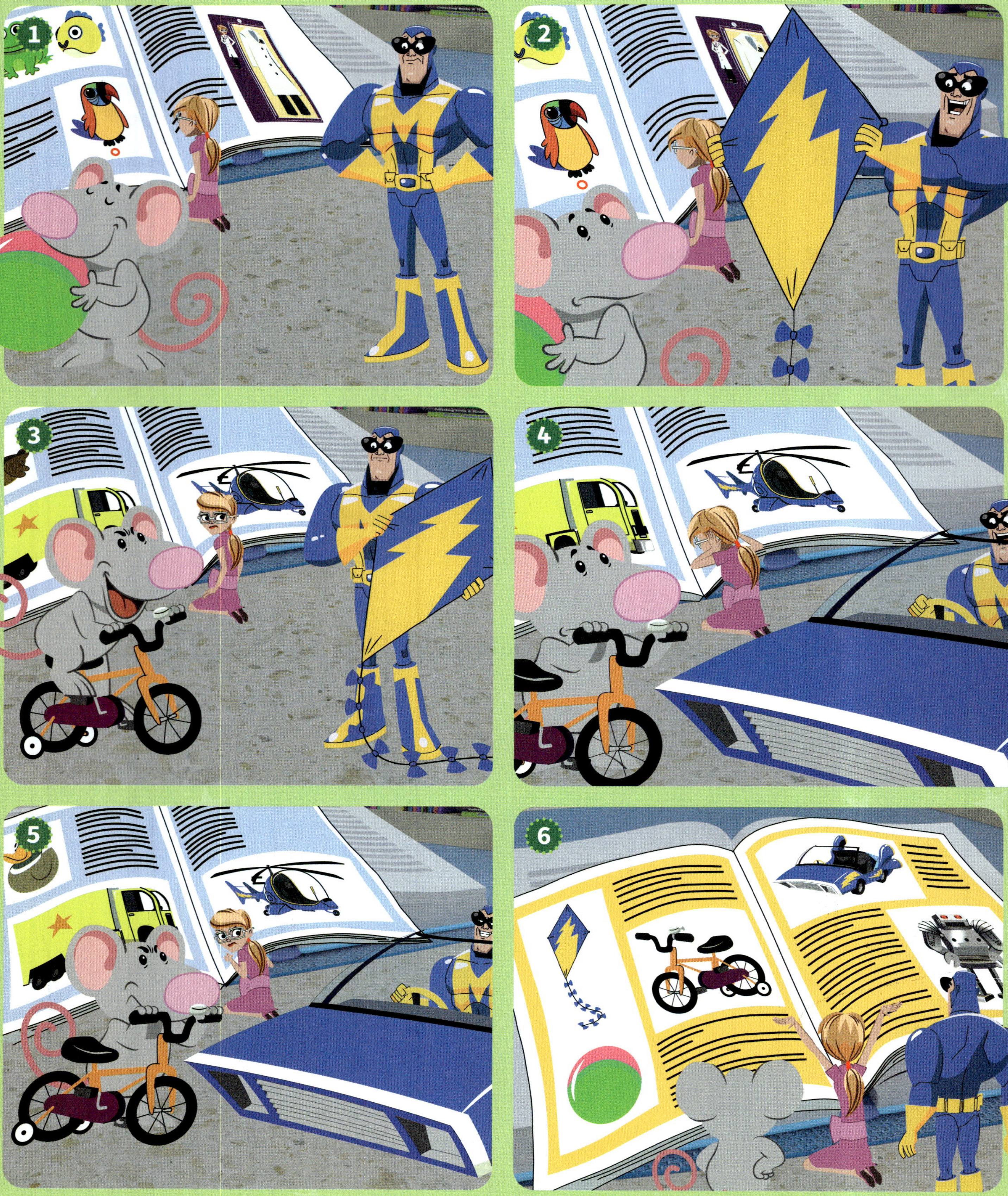

1 (89) Listen and circle. Say.

1

✓ ✗

2

✓ ✗

3

✓ ✗

4

✓ ✗

5

✓ ✗

6

✓ ✗

2 Draw a line (→ ↘ ↗). Say.

I've got five grey legs.

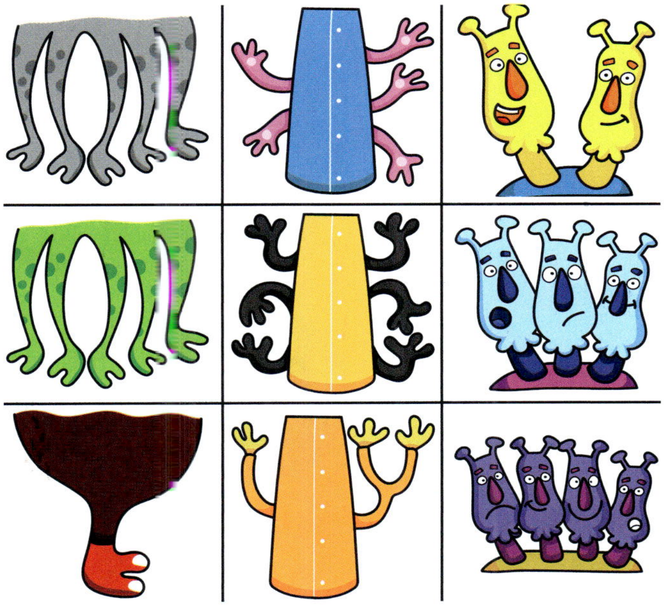

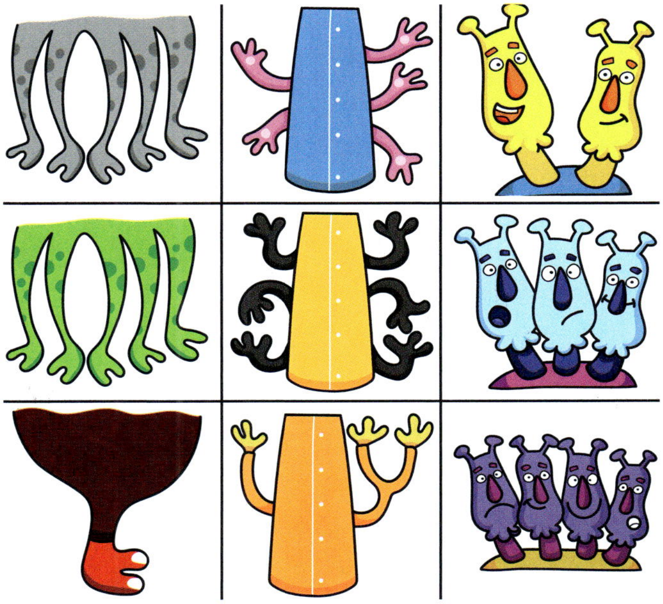

Monty's sounds

1 90 **Watch and say.**

2 **Choose, draw and say.**

I'm an egg. I've got three legs.

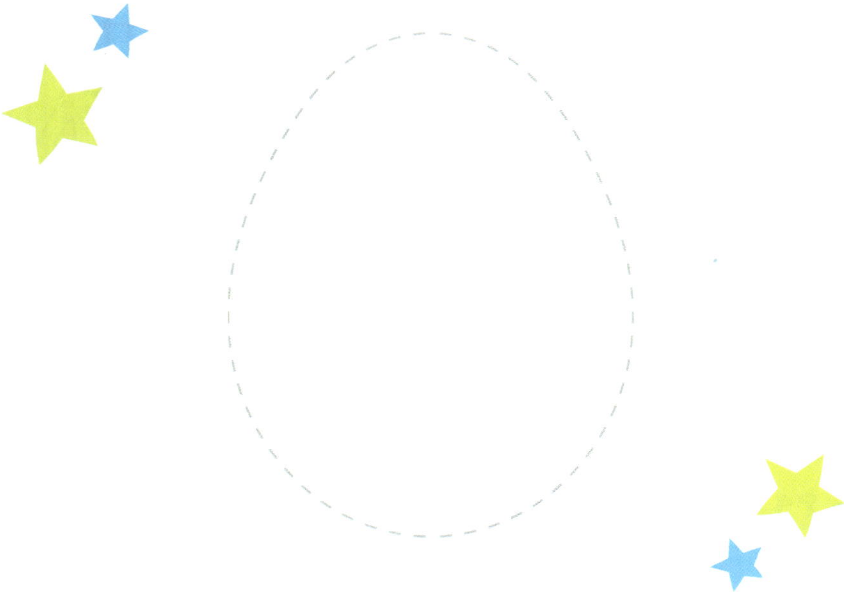

Sounds: *egg*, *bed*, *leg*, *head*

1 91 Listen and stick.

2 92 Talk to Maskman.

Marie's art

How can we make art?

1 Watch the video. Answer.

2 93 Listen and write the number. Say.

3 Look and draw lines.

1 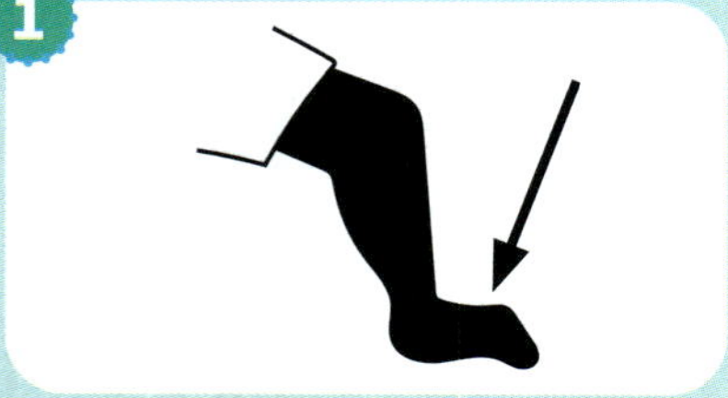

2 

3 

4 Look and say the body part. Draw.

1

2

3

4

5 Talk about art you make.

Project

Use your hands to create art.

Maskman's practice

1 94 **Listen and write the number.**

2 **Draw and colour. Say and colour.**

Where's the white ball?

It's on the table.

3 95 Listen and tick (✓) or cross (✗).

1

2

3

4

4 Choose and colour. Say and colour.

I've got red legs.

Trevor's values

Taking turns

1 96 **Listen and point.**

2 **Act it out.**

Taking turns: *Let's play pairs. OK. You start. It's my turn.* | collaboration

Review Units 5 and 6

1 97 Listen and draw lines.

1

2

3

4

2 98 Listen and circle.

1
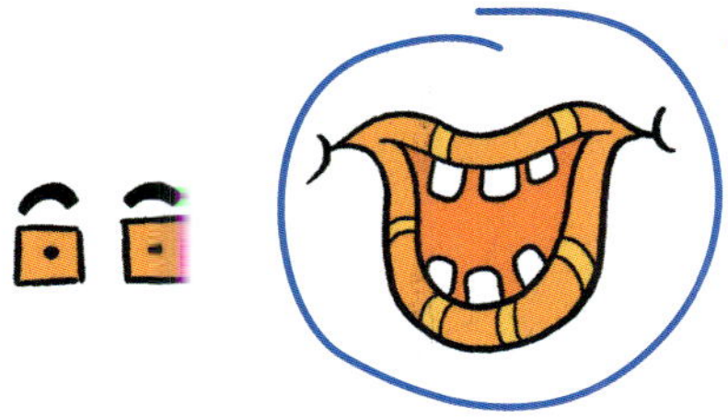
2
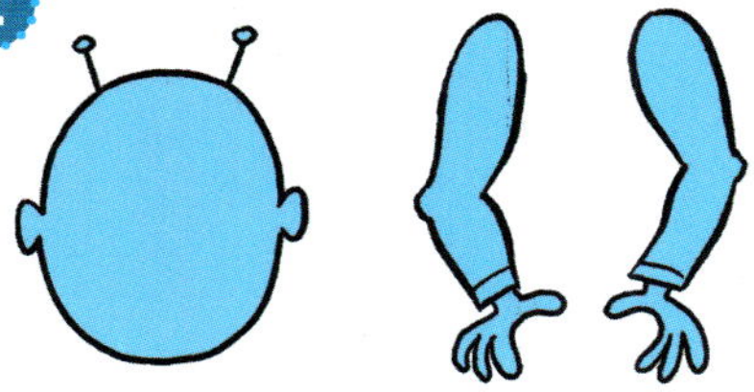
3

4
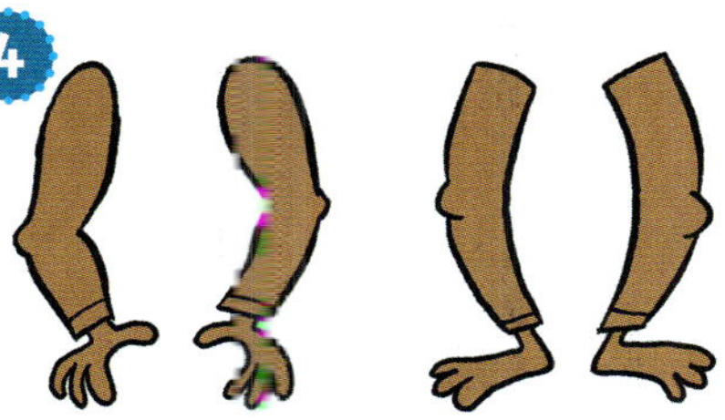
5

6
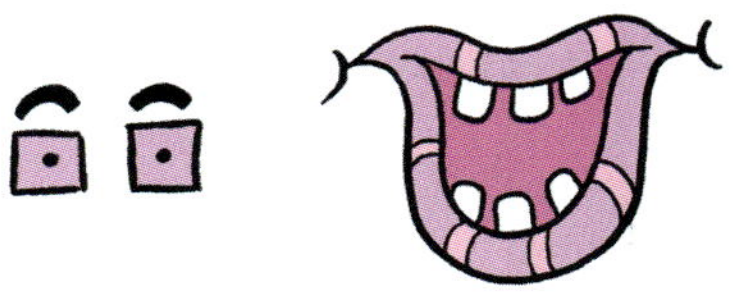

Remember to finish the online activities for these units on Practice Extra.

7 My animals

1 99–100 **Listen and point. Listen and repeat.**

2 101 **Say the chant. Do the actions.**

1 102 Listen and follow.

2 103 Listen and draw lines.

Do the online activities on Practice Extra as you complete this unit.

1 104 Listen and point. Sing the song.

2 Say and do.

Language presentation: *I can jump. I can't fly.*

1 1C6 Listen and tick (✓).

1

2

3

4

2 1C7 Listen and write the number.

1 108 Watch the video. Listen and act out the story.

1 🎧 109 Listen and draw lines.

2 Tick (✓) or cross (✗). Ask three friends.

Me				
1				
2				
3				

Monty's sounds

1 110 **Watch and say.**

2 **Ask and answer.**

Toy cats?

Two toy cats.

Sounds: *t̲wo*, *t̲igers*, *cat̲*, *t̲oys*, *not̲*

1 111 Listen and stick.

2 112 Talk to Maskman.

8 My food

1 113–114 **Listen and point. Listen and repeat.**

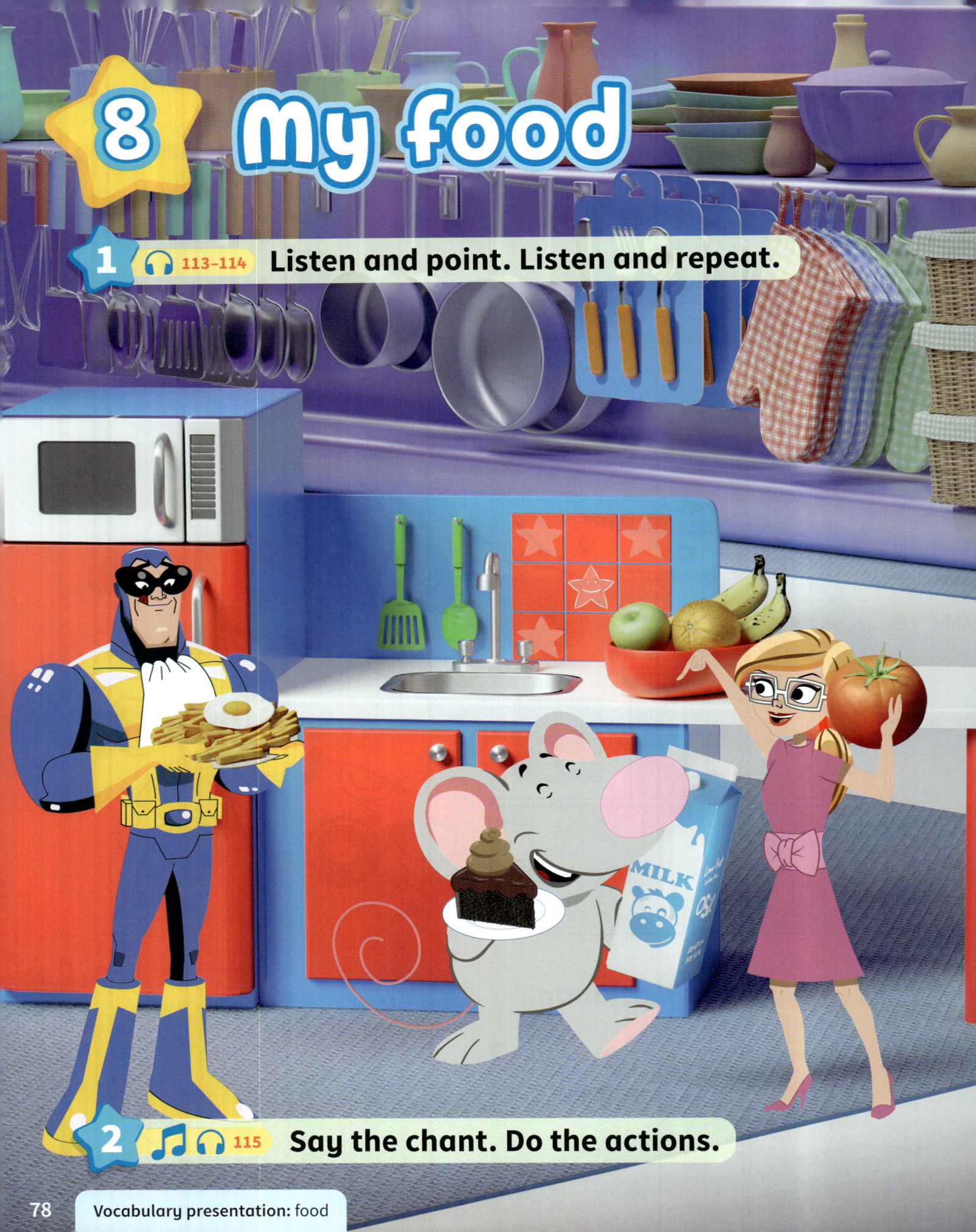

2 115 **Say the chant. Do the actions.**

1 116 Listen and circle.

1

2

3

4

5

6

2 Look and complete.

1

2

3

4

Do the online activities on Practice Extra as you complete this unit.

1 117 **Listen and point. Sing the song.**

2 **Tell your friend.**

I like fruit. I don't like milk.

Language presentation: *I like fruit. I don't like milk.*

1 Listen and write the number.

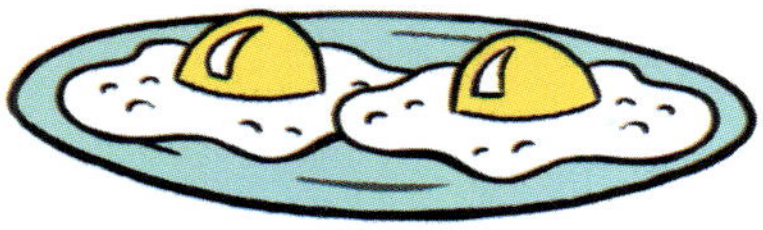

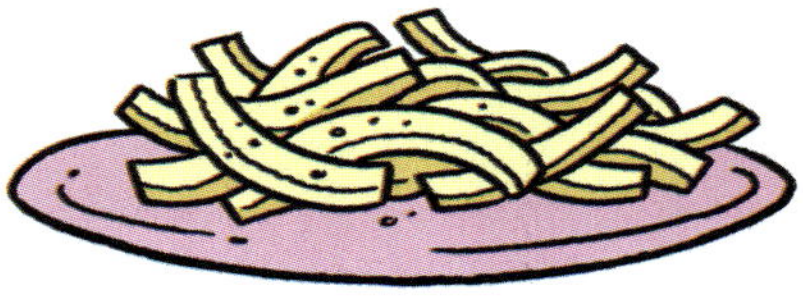

1

2 Draw food you like and don't like. Say.

Me!

Me!

1 120 Watch the video. Listen and act out the story.

1 Listen and circle. Who says it?

121

2 Draw lines. Tell your friend.

I like tomatoes.

I don't like frogs.

Monty's sounds

1 🎧 122 ▶ Watch and say.

2 Choose and say.

I like blue cake.

Sounds: *cake*, *table*, *grey*; *milk*, *pink*; *fruit*, *blue*

1 123 Listen and stick.

2 124 Talk to Maskman.

Marie's science

Is it sweet or savoury?

1 ▶ **Watch the video. Answer.**

2 🎧 125 **Listen and point. Say the words.**

3 **Look and circle.**

Sweet **Savoury**

4 116 Listen and draw lines.

1

2

5 Talk about your favourite food.

Project

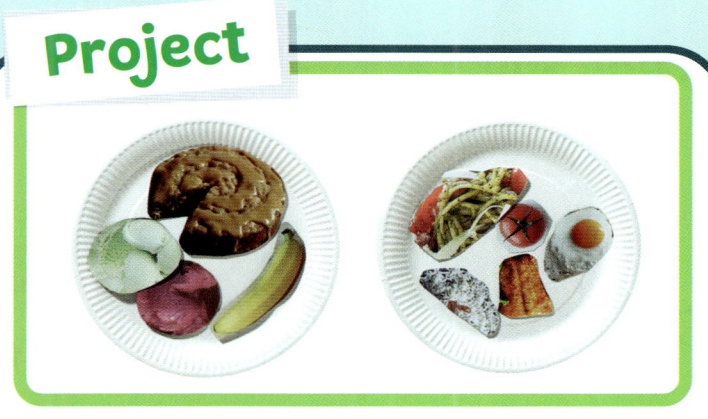

Make sweet and savoury food plates.

Maskman's practice

1 Count and write. Ask and answer.

4

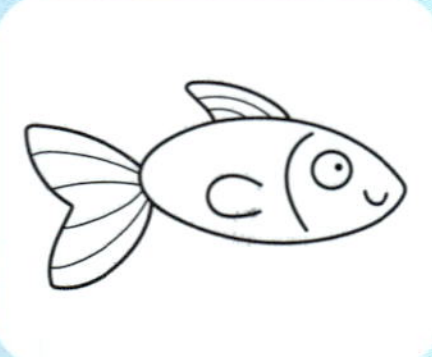

2 Point and say.

The tiger can jump. It can't fly.

3 12[illegible] Find groups of three. Draw lines. Listen and check.

1

2

3

4

4 Play and say.

I don't like kites.

I like cake.

Trevor's values

Sharing

1 128 **Listen and point.**

2 **Act it out.**

Review Units 7 and 8

1 129 Listen and colour.

2 130 Listen and draw lines.

Remember to finish the online activities for these units on Practice Extra.

Review puzzle units 1–8

4
6
5
BATH

Review game units 1–8

28
27
26
25
24
21
22
23
12
11
10
9
8
5
6
7

Thanks and Acknowledgements

Authors' thanks

Many thanks to everyone at Cambridge University Press for their dedication and hard work, and in particular to:

Liane Grainger and Lynn Townsend for supervising the whole project and guiding us calmly through the storms;

Alison Bewsher for her keen editorial eye, enthusiasm and great suggestions;

Eve Conway for great suggestions and sound editorial contribution;

We would also like to thank all our pupils and colleagues, past, present and future, at Star English academy in Murcia, especially Jim Kelly for his friendship and support throughout the years.

Dedications

For my parents, Eric and Pauline, with much love and gratitude. – CN
For Shirley and Neville, love – MT

The authors and publishers acknowledge the following sources of copyright material and are grateful for the permissions granted. While every effort has been made, it has not always been possible to identify the sources of all the material used, or to trace all copyright holders. If any omissions are brought to our notice, we will be happy to include the appropriate acknowledgements on reprinting and in the next update to the digital edition, as applicable.

Key: U = Unit

Photography

The following photos are sourced from Getty Images.

U1: Sturti/E+; Anna Erastova/iStock/Getty Images Plus; **U2:** Marcy Maloy/DigitalVision; George Doyle/Stockbyte; Diana Duzbayeva/Design Pics; Anna Erastova/iStock/Getty Images Plus; **U3:** Anna Erastova/iStock/Getty Images Plus; **U4:** ElementalImaging/E+; gwflash/iStock/Getty Images Plus; Kwanchai Lerttanapunyaporn/EyeEm; carlosalvarez/E+; Anna Erastova/iStock/Getty Images Plus; **U5:** Anna Erastova/iStock/Getty Images Plus; JoKMedia/E+; **U6:** JGI/Jamie Grill; Blend Images – Take A Pix Media; studyoritim/E+; KidStock/Photodisc; Charles Thatcher/The Image Bank/Getty Images Plus; Mrs_2015/RooM; Anna Erastova/iStock/Getty Images Plus; **U7:** Anna Erastova/iStock/Getty Images Plus; **U8:** Tetra Images – Jamie Grill/Brand X Pictures; Westend61; Kiana Rosalez/EyeEm; fotosr/iStock/Getty Images Plus; jayk7/Moment; asikkk/iStock/Getty Images Plus; Anna Erastova/iStock/Getty Images Plus.

The following photos are sourced from other libraries.

U2: Oleg Beloborodov/Alamy Stock Photo; **U4:** RTimages/Alamy Stock Photo; **U6:** SpeedKingz/Shutterstock; **U8:** Silatip/Shutterstock.

Commissioned photography by Copy cat.

Illustrations

Blooberry (source Pronk Media Inc.); Copy cat; Beatrice Costamagna, c/o Pickled Ink; Chris Jones; Helen Naylor, c/o Plum Pudding; Kelly Kennedy, c/o Sylvie Poggio; Melanie Sharp, c/o Sylvie Poggio; Richard Hoit, Beehive; Xian Xio, c/o IllustrationWeb; Pronk Media Inc.; Jake Mcdonald, c/o The Bright Agency; Marek Jagucki; Matthew Scott.

Cover illustrations by Pronk Media Inc.

Audio

Audio production by Creative Listening.

Video

Video acknowledgements are in the Teacher Resources on Cambridge One.

Design and typeset

Design and typeset by Blooberry Design

Additional authors

Katy Kelly: Monty's Sounds

Rebecca Legros: Marie's maths, art and science

Freelance editor

Stephanie Howard

1 Hello! (page 11)

2 My class (page 19)

3 My colours (page 33)

4 My toys (page 41)

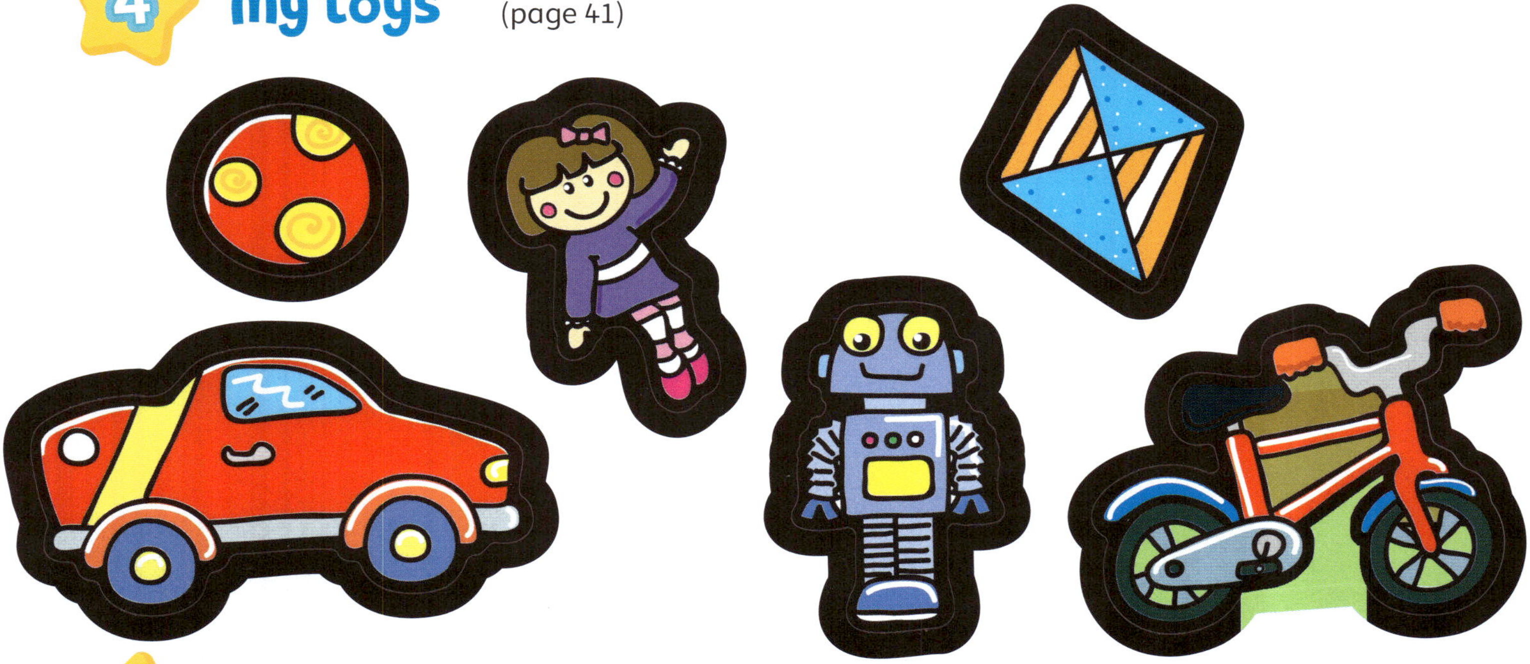

Talk to Maskman

5 My house (page 55)

6 My body (page 63)

7 My animals

(page 77)

8 My food

(page 85)

Talk to Maskman